LESSONS LEARNED

LESSONS LEARNED

Stories of a Teacher and Teaching

David M. Becker

JOSEPH H. ZUMBALEN PROFESSOR
OF THE LAW OF PROPERTY EMERITUS
WASHINGTON UNIVERSITY SCHOOL OF LAW

CAROLINA ACADEMIC PRESS
Durham, North Carolina

ISBN   978-1-5310-1511-4
e-ISBN   978-1-5310-1512-1

Library of Congress Cataloging-in-Publication Data

Names: Becker, David M., 1935- author.
Title: Lessons learned / by David M. Becker.
Description: Durham, North Carolina : Carolina Academic Press, LLC, 2019. |
    Includes bibliographical references and index.
Identifiers: LCCN 2019006343 | ISBN 9781531015114 (alk. paper)
Subjects: LCSH: Lawyers--Fiction. | Law schools--Fiction. | Law
    students--Fiction. | Legal stories.
Classification: LCC PS3602.E2893 L47 2019 | DDC 813/.6--dc23
LC record available at https://lccn.loc.gov/2019006343

Carolina Academic Press
700 Kent Street
Durham, NC 27701
Telephone (919) 489-7486
Fax (919) 493-5668
www.cap-press.com

Printed in the United States of America

For my students from whom I have learned much, and in memory of two among them—Stuart Oelbaum and Chaitanya Maddali.

CONTENTS

PREFACE

This book is about lessons learned (both conferred and received) by a fictitious protagonist, E. Randall Mann, who had been a law teacher at a major law school for over fifty years. There are nine stories or chapters that comprise this book. The stories appear as written in the first person by Mann and a fictitious student, Billie Williams, who served as his research assistant after he had retired and ultimately wrote two of the stories in remembrance following Mann's death. Although the context for lessons learned is law school and legal education, the lessons are intended to be transcendent. They explore the complex ingredients of life that often enrich us all. Courage. Resilience and Survival. Introspection, Self-Knowledge and Awareness. Death and Loss. Race. Trust. Friendship. Love. And above all Inspiration.

Despite the appearance of Mann and Williams as authors, I am the true author and, like Mann, a law teacher for over fifty years. To be sure, this book could have been written differently; for example, in the third person or as nonfiction. And if fiction, I could have appeared as the protagonist as well as the author. Yet this book of stories is not an embellished autobiography, an inference by readers I want studiously to avoid. Certainly, the lessons learned are lessons I embrace. Nevertheless, I firmly believe that only fiction allowed me to depart from personal experience and real life, and to disguise and borrow from others, and especially to completely fabricate. Best of all, it offered the joy and freedom to let conversations among characters take me in unexpected directions that led to new insights, new twists, better stories, and heightened messages for life and living. Something legal writing for over fifty years never allowed.

So I hope you enjoy these stories, because I loved every moment in creating them.

David M. Becker
April 2019

LESSONS LEARNED

CHAPTER 1

MY SUMMER AS RESEARCH ASSISTANT TO PROFESSOR E. RANDALL MANN

Billie Williams

January 25, 2009

Dear Ms. Williams:

I hope you are doing very well and enjoying your Spring Semester classes. I also assume that you are working on summer plans. I know that you don't know me. Although now retired, I have been a teacher at the Eliot University School of Law for fifty years. Do you have any interest in applying for a Summer Research Position with me? You have been highly recommended. This coming summer I have only one position to fill. The pay is low ($14/hr for 450 hours of work), the hours are flexible (no rigid times to punch in or out), and the dress code is non-existent, and I hope there is some fun along the way. If interested, we can discuss the position and what it entails on the phone. Although I am out-of-town at the moment, I am generally reachable by e-mail (Mann@Eliot.edu), at school (935-744-0000) or cell phone (935-745-0000). If you wish to apply, please let me know and also attach your resume.

Sincerely,

E. Randall Mann
W.Y. Eliot Professor Emeritus of Property Law

This was my introduction to Professor Mann. The e-mail came out of the clear blue while I was studying in the library. I had just begun my second semester at the Eliot School of Law. My first reaction was "who the hell is Mann." I leaned over and asked a classmate in the carrel next to me. She replied: "Oh he's that guy who has been around forever, is the oldest in the building, and has his name on plaques and scholarships everywhere."

I should have known or at least recalled; his name was on my full ride through law school, but was that the reason for this invitation? I had done very well my first semester; I had always done very well in school. Essentially A's throughout, always first (or near it) in the class, class valedictorian and president. School was easy, something I was good at and could count on. So was athletics. Basketball was my game, four-year point guard, and always a captain, letter winner, and more. I had attended and played for Eliot University, graduated four years earlier, taught school, and worked in public relations. And now I knew what I really wanted to do, or so I thought.

Even though I had worked for four years after graduation, I had no clear idea as to what I wanted out of law school, or why I even came to law school. I never admitted the latter to anyone, not my parents, best friends, or even myself. I said all the right things, including wanting to make the world a better place. The law and lawyering, and things related to it, seemed to be as good an explanation as anything to do exactly that. But making the world better never seemed comfortable; it simply wasn't me. And once I entered law school, doing good—a familiar theme for many—quickly got lost, forgotten, or rejected. Debt stood in the way for many and big time jobs displaced doing good for others. For many in betweeners, it was the grind of daily cases, statutes, nuanced and meticulous reading, abstract and complicated analysis of rules and policy, and classroom interrogation that left you numbed, embattled, knocked down, and sometimes crippled with insecurity, so much so that you stopped caring about the end game and simply wanted to survive. As to the latter, although it took a while for self-realization to show up, I recognized that was my magnet for law school. Competition and survival of the best. I knew I could compete at most anything and with the best, and my immediate and long range goals were always driven by wanting to be the best. Quite simply, at the Eliot School of Law, I would be up against the best and could prove once again that I could climb to the mountain top faster than anyone. And at the end of one semester, I was poised to conquer all.

I had received my first semester's grades merely a week before Professor Mann's e-mail; four out of four courses with A+'s that assured me a rank near the top of the class. They were complete confirmation of me, my admission, scholarship and living stipend, as well as my past and future. They were my ticket to a good job and good life. After all, first semester grades drove everything: a summer job at the end of the school year with a large firm and handsome pay. And that job, and its performance, set up a second summer job, followed by a permanent offer following graduation. Second semester grades could be influential but were usually inconsequential. My initial reaction to the e-mail was disinterest, actually something more—disdain. Who needed him at $14 an hour when the job I coveted and now had earned and deserved paid $2,000 a week? Mann's e-mail asked for a reply, but I did not. Instead, I tapped the delete button and returned to preparation for next day's class in criminal law.

A week later, the entire 1-L class met with the Director of the Career Services Office to discuss the market for summer jobs, search strategies, on campus interviews with law firms, and all the ways CSO could provide assistance. But the dark cloud was saved for last. We all had heard about it, but few really understood or appreciated its consequences, short and long-term. No one thought it would affect them because every law student expected to be among the elite at the top of their class, and that kind of academic success was a ticket to good high paying jobs despite the onset of the great recession. The dark cloud was a reality check. The legal profession was undergoing significant change, and the immediate consequence was a contraction of lawyers and staff that began with summer internships which for some firms were being reduced to ZERO. At one point in assessing the job market for the summer, the Director said: "Some of you will get an offer to work for a law professor, and my advice is to seize it. Research positions are important work experiences, and they look great on your resume."

My classmates were alarmed, even those at the very top of the class. Interviews for summer internships with large firms were two months away, and opportunities for actual high paying jobs had become uncertain at best. Absent those jobs, I would have to knock on law office doors of small firms in hope that my timing was right with someone who would probably pay me less than $14 an hour or even the money I might make waiting tables. So I went to my deleted file and immediately e-mailed the four previous RAs listed by Mann in a follow-up e-mail for consultation in making my decision. Within several days I heard from all four and spoke at length with two. There was a consensus among them about specifics and overall experiences. Each recommended I apply and accept the position immediately, partly because of the experience and mostly because of the shrinking market for jobs with law firms. The work usually involved two articles he was writing, one that was approaching completion and the other in its earliest stage. And they usually focused on the law of property or legal education. Mann himself, however, seemed to be the best part. He was quirky, long-winded, friendly, interested and interesting, could sometimes read your mind, knew throughout the U.S. thousands of lawyers and many judges well, loved to talk about them and tell stories (often boring), and could probably assure you a good job in whatever market you wanted. Additionally, he took you to lunch weekly, and often with former students who were judges and leading lawyers at law firms, corporations, or the government who discussed what they did and why they enjoyed it. Best of all, these lunches with former students amounted to a head start on landing interviews and outstanding jobs. Given this description, I quickly concluded that it was time to play defense, not offense, in finding a job for the summer.

So I returned to my delete file, found his e-mail, replied, and told Professor Mann that I was interested in applying for the summer position especially after having consulted with his former RAs, that I had attached my resume, and that I looked forward to hearing from him. The next day I heard from him: "Let's speak on the phone. I have your phone number off of your resume and you have mine. What time should I call?"

I immediately replied: "How about tonight at 8?"

Moments later: "I will call you then."

And at 8:00 sharp, my phone rang. After answering and responding "Hello," I heard: "May I call you Billie because I would like you to call me Randy." Although still winter, that was the beginning of my "summer experience with E. Randall Mann."

His voice was raspy, then and throughout, that was a clear indicator of his age, early eighties. There was vitality and enthusiasm in his questions and his responses to mine. It was an easy and comfortable conversation. The work for the summer would involve an article already underway that focused on the Rule in Wild's Case. (I told him I knew nothing about it. He replied that few did, including teachers, and that regarding this project, ignorance on the subject was an advantage not a disadvantage.) He also added that I would be working on a second article critical of contemporary higher education. Additionally, he discussed his obligatory lunches often with guests. Mann acknowledged that the pay was low, that he wanted to keep me well-fed, and also establish a network for landing a job. Mann then asked what questions I might have. I reiterated that a lot had already been answered by his former RAs, but I did want more specifics about his articles, which he then joyfully explained, giving me more than I wanted to know at that moment. Just when I thought our interview had come to an end, he said: "I have a few more important questions for you."

"OK," I said.

"Do you have a sense of humor?"

I was surprised by the question and waited for what seemed an eternity before saying simply "Yes." But I knew deep down that was a failed answer. Before he could say anything more, I added: "I am in my late twenties but into many things created before I was born. I love Saturday Night Live and watch it every week, and everything Tina Fey has done. I own video copies of Sid Caesar and Imogene Cocoa. I like Marx brothers' movies — and Woody Allen too — and To Bet Your Life with Groucho. And I own a copy of the Blues Brothers and also Citizen Kane."

"Citizen Kane?" he exclaimed.

"Gotcha," I said, and got him I did.

Mann then asked: "Do you play tennis?"

"Better than you," I said.

He paused and then simply said: "The job is yours if you want it. How long do you need to make your decision, because if you cannot decide soon, I will have to look elsewhere?"

And then I surprised myself with an immediate response: "I accept, so when do I begin?"

We then got into nuts and bolts involving information needed by the business office, spring time exams, and a convenient time to commence work thereafter, and more immediately, a luncheon date with Mann and previous RAs after he returned to town. The RAs would have lots of advice on conducting research for me, who were the best luncheon guests to follow up with, and how to make this a worthwhile summer on cheap wages. As to a begin date, he urged me to enter the competition for a place on the law reviews that immediately followed exams and to take a brief vacation thereafter if wanted and convenient. But he also told me that I could interrupt the summer at any time to get away or simply play. All of this was easy enough and seemed to make sense.

The meeting with the RAs went well, I took my final exams and firmly believed I aced them, and then competed for a law review position expecting an invitation to the number one journal. After that, without opting for vacation, work began, first with the Rule in Wild's Case. Within a few days, Mann arranged for lunch, just the two of us. He arrived in cargo shorts, a well-worn t-shirt, sunglasses, and tennis shoes. At one time, I was sure, Mann exceeded 6 feet tall. But not then. He was hunched over particularly when walking almost as if he was leaning forward while ascending a hill. One leg was bowed and the other was straight with a long scar that must have covered up a knee replacement. His face was relatively unlined and shaven. And the fingers on his hands appeared as if broken numerous times. The little hair on his scalp seemed rearranged to hide significant baldness, yet without success because of patches that had a mind of their own and gave him the appearance of a mad scientist. I quickly discovered that he did not do quick or inexpensive lunches. The restaurant was French. I had heard of it before but never been there. Mann enjoyed good food at good restaurants with good service and good ambience, and when possible to sit outside and linger. And he loved to talk, often too much and too long. He simply enjoyed conversation about anything and everything. He had opinions but was not opinionated because he always insisted on discovering the views of others, dealt with them respectfully, and was open to persuasion and conversion. Except when it came to sports. Professor Mann was an unabashed and diehard Chicago Cubs fan who claimed he attended a game when they last appeared in the World Series but not the last time they won the World Series. He was hopelessly optimistic and could not understand others who discounted and derided his Cubbies. This was his blind spot, his only one, and never enough to make the summer intolerable.

The first lunch of the summer was devoted to a primer on the Rule in Wild's Case and other ambiguous dispositive word patterns that had appeared in deeds, trusts, and wills that courts tried to interpret consistently but, according to Mann, without justification. It soon became clear that the article wasn't really about simply the Rule in Wild's Case; instead, it was about precedent and the merits of deviating from it. After that background to my main research project, Mann wanted to know about me. "Tell me about yourself, Billie." After reciting and elaborating on things appearing in my resume, which he had read carefully, Mann stopped me: "No, really tell me about you. What makes you 'hum'?"

"Professor what do you mean? Hum?"

"Billie, I heard that expression first from a brilliant novelist. Some might say 'what makes you tick,' but he felt 'hum' meant many things and clearly something more. What kinds of things inspire interest, better yet passion? What drives you? What do you make of life and what you want to do with it? Billie, all the big questions and thoughts that enter our minds and sometimes keep us awake at night!"

"Professor, I am not sure I have these thoughts, or at least have consciously focused upon them."

"Billie, that's nonsense. We all have them, even as young children; for example, 'why are my parents fighting, is it because they hate me,' or 'will I ever grow to be tall enough to be a great basketball player'? The shape, content, and contour of these thoughts, of course, evolves over time. I must confess that at my age sickness and death is at the center of everything."

"Professor, how much time do I have to think about this or to respond?"

"Billie, we have the entire summer."

Our second lunch was at Mann's favorite Italian restaurant, and, after asking whether I was hungry, he insisted I order several courses, including anything on the menu even if it meant leftovers to take home.

"Professor, you asked me to call you Randy, but at certain moments Professor is much easier."

"That's OK with me so long as you never use Professor while we are on the tennis courts."

"OK, that's a deal. Also, I may have an answer to your big question — what makes me hum."

"So, Billie? I am waiting."

"Professor, at my core is competition and success at it. I guess it's written all over me and everything I do. I can't attribute that to family and upbringing, it's just something that's always underscored interest and over the top motivation."

"Billie, is that what brings you to law and law school?"

"I think so. In redirecting my life after nearly four years out of college, I settled on being a lawyer by default. But I did think about it further. Doing good seemed more respectable, yet once in law school and surrounded by others truly committed to public service, I recognized that law school and the practice are about competition. And that suited me just fine. I knew I could compete, and success at it would make me hum."

Mann did not respond to my revelation immediately or directly. We ordered appetizers, and I soon discovered how much he loved calamari fried, grilled, marinated, or however. After that it was a salad. But I don't honestly recall what we discussed during that interval. Thinking back, we may have said very little because later that summer he talked about one of his favorite mystery writers, an Italian whose books were translated into English and focused on a Sicilian inspector/detective who loved food, loved elaborate lunches, and devoted that time to enjoy great food, think, and even solve the crime at hand. Above all, however, Mann had to eat slowly, for me often painfully, and in silence. Like the Inspector, he believed that elegant meals must be savored and conversation could only interfere. After that I observed there were always periods of silence, sometimes prolonged, at each of our lunches even after guests were added. But I do recall the specific conversation at our second lunch when the time arrived for espresso and dolce.

"Now then," Mann began. It was almost as if he had lost sight of his prolonged moments of silence and viewed our dialogue as uninterrupted. "Is that competition you say? Or do you mean challenges? Or both?"

"No Professor, I think it is competition; going up against adversaries and the exhilaration of victory, success, and being the best or among them. It's what I always have gotten out of sports and, in particular, basketball. I thrive on the preparation, practice, hard work, and ultimately the huge pay-off that accompanies the effort."

We then sipped our espressos slowly and respectfully and tasted an assortment of gelati, which were the best I ever had. He paid the check, we got in his car, and while returning to school, Mann said: "Billie, so you intend to become a litigator" with an inflection converting his declaration into a question.

"Why do you say that Professor? I have liked all my courses thus far except for Civil Procedure, which is a must for litigators."

Mann thought for a moment, and then he simply asked: "After graduation from law school, where is the ongoing competition for you as a lawyer? What's the next level?"

"I suppose, Professor, it's the fast track to partnership at a top law firm."

"And after that?"

"What do you mean Professor?"

"Billie, where is the next competition? Is it the race for more and more money or power, an endless race that may not have anything to do with merit but instead politics?"

"Goodness, no!"

"Billie, that's what every idealistic law student says. No, then what is it? And where is it? Another law firm and another ascendancy? Billie, litigation is where it's at, there are always winners and losers at least in the eyes of so-called winners even when settled. Yes, other areas of law invite competition like corporate takeovers and mergers and acquisitions. But with litigation, Billie, competition is a constant and that's you."

"Professor, I guess I had better learn to love Civil Procedure and master it along with Evidence, Trial Practice, and other related courses."

"One more thing, Billie. You want competition, but does winning underlie everything? Would competition be satisfying and make you hum without victory?"

"Professor, what do you mean?"

"What I mean is that competition in the courtroom yields winners and losers, just like basketball, tennis, and you name the sport."

Before he could begin his next sentence, I interrupted: "What's wrong with competing to be THE VICTOR?"

"Billie, when I was a young practicing lawyer recently graduated from law school, I met a legendary criminal defense lawyer. I had read about him and had followed his work in the courtroom long before law school. He was African-American, a solo practitioner, with a two room office on Chicago's South Side. His winning percentage in trials was near 100, and almost all involved homicides. When I met him, he was in his eighties, just like me today, still practicing, and still a winner. Looking back I was awe struck. 'Mr. Green, what's the secret of your extraordinary record? How have you been able to accomplish this?' He replied: 'Young man, it's simple, you've got to confine your cases to winners only. In my part of the city, there are bars and lots of Saturday night disputes that result in death, typically between two men involving a woman. Bystanders don't like the police and don't talk. The victim is dead and my client is alive, and seldom is there anyone around to contest his side of the story. Simple as that. Winning is good but no great feat.' Billie, if you want repeated victories, just find the right niche with easy pickings for victories. But over time it will be without challenges and probably satisfaction. Just ask any civil rights lawyer, from the 1960s and certainly before, about life without constant victory. Remember 'winning is good but no great feat.' And the practice of law is, hopefully, for a lifetime of many years. You may have to look for sustenance beyond victory."

There was a pause, but I did not respond. Finally, Mann broke the silence. "Billie, one more thing, although I should forewarn you I always have one more thing or things. Think of life ahead with me. After graduation. Then five years into practice, ten years, fifteen years, twenty, and thereafter. While in school, your victories come with grades, class rank, editor-in-chief of the law review, coif, and other awards. Afterwards, what then? In practice, is it partner, then equity partner? Assuming you want litigation and can't cherry pick your cases, what do you do about the cases you lose or settle to stave off further losses? Where are your rewards; your nourishment for preparation and hard work? Or what if you find yourself representing a corporation that is negotiating purchase of another and, at your client's instruction, you construct the best deal possible along with supporting documents, and then the deal breaks down because it wasn't a good one to begin with or instead your client simply changes its mind? And worst of all, your client wants you to cut your bill reflecting many hours of preparation and hard work in half or refuses to pay at all because the deal has evaporated so the company cannot profit by it and neither should you. Again, where are your good grades and your proclamations of victory or proxies for success? They are clear-cut now and for the immediate future, but will they be there for your professional lifetime?"

I had no response. We returned to the law school and Mann said "farewell until next week's lunch with a special guest." I went to my work station, a small office for several RAs, sat there devastated and silent, and then I picked up and left for my apartment. I was through for the day. Within a few hours my feelings turned to anger. Who the hell does he think he is? Mann asks me a big question, not about work or school in particular, but about me; a question that is personal and involves a subject few people my age probe, and he expects an answer along with discussion. So I give him one that's honest and I thought would suit him and be more than enough. But no, all it did was invite more questions, always just one more, combined with unrelenting lecture. How dare him! I signed on for legal research and not psychiatric analysis. By the end of the following weekend I was ready to resign and search for a law job or wait tables. He was retired, and his deadlines were entirely self-imposed, so abandoning him would be no big thing. Then again, maybe it would. I didn't know him well enough to know whether he could be vindictive. And whether or not working for him for a short time, and then quitting, appeared on my resume, it would be difficult to hide. So I decided to soldier on and do my best to avoid the big questions and, if unavoidable, to provide answers that ended the discussion.

The third lunch was with a lawyer, Joan Saltwater, who had graduated thirty-five years ago when she was one of just several women in a class of one hundred fifty. Joan was clearly among Mann's "all-time favorites" even though he used that expression frequently. She was a brilliant lawyer who specialized in employee benefits; but even more important for me, Joan thought a lot about what lawyers do and how they could do it well and simultaneously lead a balanced life. And she had written about it and published a book that laid out critical precepts for good lawyering with rules as simple and obvious as return all phone calls SOON, don't order red sauce or artichokes at a business lunch, be respectful of staff, especially your assistant or the assistants of clients and even opposing counsel because they can make you or break you or both, or as sophisticated as learn how to control the tempo of critical meetings and negotiations because those who control tempo control the deal. She also focused on me. Although she wanted to know a lot about me, she did not ask Mann's kind of "big" question. Instead, she was practically oriented. What firms locally or elsewhere and what kind of work interested me? She reviewed my resume carefully, suggested changes, talked about interviewing and offered a formal rehearsal with her. Additionally, Joan stated she would arrange an interview later that summer with her office, a large, well-known, prestigious firm located in six major markets within the U.S. Throughout lunch, Mann said nothing but smiled frequently, often as if to punctuate everything Joan was saying. Afterwards we returned to school together in silence, and then parted with once again Mann's remark of "farewell until next week at lunch with another guest."

But this time I replied: "Joan was terrific, and I very much appreciated meeting her." And I did. Without more, meeting Joan, and weekly others like her, seemed to justify the summer experience and a decision not to flee.

But the next day, the bottom dropped out as my life and its direction were abruptly and significantly turned upside down. I received my grades for the second semester. It felt like total failure as to myself and my courses. The latter was not literally true; nevertheless, that's the way I felt. After one semester of law school, I had been in the top one percent, and after one full year, I had fallen to just inside the cut-off for the top quarter. This was territory I had never known my entire life, and I hated it. It felt undeserved, unfair, maybe even discriminatory by whom and against what did not matter. I also felt cheated by the other students who had leapfrogged above me and now occupied class ranks meant for me. They hadn't earned it as I had, especially those whose academic history hadn't matched mine and certainly those who had attended inferior colleges and universities. They had wrongfully stolen my destiny. The next day I was ready to leave school, called home, and vented endlessly to both parents. But by the next, I had settled down a bit and went to Professor Mann's office to request cancellation of the following Tuesday lunch.

His door was open and he greeted me warmly. I began by requesting cancellation of lunch, and he asked why. I was determined to hold back tears, but I could not hold off emotion. So I quickly related my grades, rank, and confrontation with academic and lifetime disaster. Mann listened carefully. After a strategic and Mann-like silence, he said "Billie, I have a question, just one."

"Professor, not that again."

"Yes, Billie—did you ever know that I saw you play basketball for Eliot University? In fact, many times?"

"No, but so what?"

"Billie, it was my favorite game to play until my early seventies and still is my favorite to watch. I regularly attended the home games of men and women. Frankly I enjoyed the women best of all. They play the game the way it was meant to be played. Crisp passes, well executed plays, selfless basketball. I loved it and still attend."

"Professor, I had no idea."

"Yes, Billie, and I truly enjoyed watching you play the game. You were terrific. The best point guard I have seen at Eliot. You controlled the ball and the game. You saw the floor, directed your teammates, made the right passes, and did it with ease and calm. You shot well from out and could go all the way to the basket. And best of all, you made free throws, especially when the game was on the line. Billie you displayed talent, moxie, and above all GRIT. You did it in games you won easily, and from behind, and in those you lost. It was always front and center, plain old fashioned GRIT!"

"Professor Mann, I am flattered—I absolutely am—by your description of me as a basketball player. But it doesn't seem to help or make my pain disappear. Grit or no grit, I am devastated and really down. You can't imagine what's been going through my mind, including leaving school. I have even asked: 'Why has God done this to me?' And I am not an especially religious person! Yet why me? I have never failed like this before. I don't like it one bit. It's not fair!"

Again, there was a period of silence until Mann asked: "Billie, do you want a response or for me to remain quiet without adding my two cents? You can have it either way?"

"Professor, thus far, I haven't wanted or liked your unsolicited lectures. Yet I guess I'm here for a reason, and it's not simply to cancel out on lunch. I just hope you include a 'spoon full of sugar' in this lecture 'to make the medicine go down.'"

"Billie, you have been very fortunate to have never suffered serious academic disappointment. But life is not filled with the kind of 'fairness' you have experienced and come to always expect. I am certain that along the way to law school, many of your previous classmates have asked the same question: why me? You, perhaps more than anyone, must know that in sports and academic competition, as well as in much of life itself, there are no entitlements to uninterrupted success, especially as one ascends the ladder of intense competition. Billie, you are now in the major leagues, and nearly all of your classmates have had your level of success in school and your great expectations for law school and the future. Quite honestly, I don't feel sorry for you for one moment — NOT ONE BIT — and you shouldn't either! It would be different if you were on the verge of real failure — FLUNKING OUT! But you are not. You are not only in good standing, you are in great standing. Top quarter and almost unlimited opportunity is still yours if you want it. So get with it and make the most of what you have accomplished and what lies ahead.

"Oh, by the way Billie, just one more thing. If you want to improve upon this last semester, there are things to be done. Many people who have gone through this simply sulk, become resigned to their class rank, and do nothing. It takes courage, however, to really find out whether you can do better. And you can; nearly everyone does. Success at exams requires a skill set just like critical analysis and problem solving which, at its core, are what legal education is about. Experience yields improvement, but to stay ahead of the curve, you must work at it especially after discovering the weaknesses revealed in your second semester exams. There may be important clues in the responses you receive. Some may lead to fine tuning and others considerably more. But you must do your utmost to find out, and that requires conferring with your teachers in these courses. Even the ones in which you did well. It's important to learn what you did badly, but equally important to discover the kinds of things you did well and must repeat again and again. More grit Billie, GRIT.

"Oh yes Billie I am not quite finished, there is one more thing, and probably it is most important of all. It's the end game. Know yourself and what you have accomplished; it's the grade you must always give to you, your work, and your life. Victories, good grades, awards, and honors don't always exist, and those that do have a short life-span. As I once said, think ahead fifteen to twenty years, after you are a partner and well-established, what do you do to replace these metrics? Is it money, book of business, or power? Who is there to constantly reward you with a 'job well done'? Sometimes it's the client, but not always. The fact is, Billie, there is no constant source of other-directed approval. It must come from within. You, above all, must know deep-down the quality of your effort and what you have accomplished. Billie — it always begins with you. And this is also true for the present, starting today. Yes, it applies to the courses and exams you take and even the papers you write. You must know for yourself the quality of your effort in each course. You must know when you walk into your final exam what you have accomplished. The final exams and grades teachers give are, at best, imperfect measures of what you have achieved as a student and predictors of what you will achieve as a professional. For one thing, they do not and cannot test integrity, judgment, and trust, each a critical component of professional success. And for sure they do not test GRIT. Billie, I am confident that you felt good about yourself and what you had accomplished as you entered each of your second semester exams. And that was a reflection of effort, some feedback, and not arrogance. Above all, that self-judgment is your real grade and your lasting grade. As for your teacher's grade, if you receive one that leaves you in good standing, or better the top half, or even better the top quarter, that's great certainly in the long-run. You will be a lawyer and a good one, and if you don't allow others to direct your measures of satisfaction, you may also be a happy one."

I sat there numb as I was trying to listen and absorb what Mann was saying, but I wasn't certain I was really listening as I was trying to sort things out. Among other things, Mann had challenged me to do better and succeed. Somehow he knew that I would not shrink from challenges, and that was his hook. So I thanked him for listening and for his advice. And then I left quietly. Mann stood up, looked me in the eye and said: "Billie, I am NOT cancelling our Tuesday lunch with our guest."

As I walked to the door I simply replied: "I'll be there." By the time I returned to my apartment, I knew I was not withdrawing from school. Mann had thrown down a challenge I had to accept, because if I didn't, then I would know I was a real failure, something I could never live with.

The following week Mann e-mailed me with a simple message: "How about some tennis against an old man?"

I was feeling better about many things, especially after my positive and encouraging exam conferences with second semester teachers. So I replied: "You're on, where and when?" We agreed to meet the next day at 10:30 in his office and then walk over to the University tennis courts.

When I arrived, his door was open, and he was waiting. I took one look and could not contain laughter. "Randy—you told me 'Professor' was off limits on the tennis courts and I assume that includes on the way there as well—you wear more wraps than a Mummy! Is there any part of you not in pain or under repair? I didn't bargain for this, especially if it means mouth-to-mouth resuscitation or a trip to the emergency room."

"Ha ha, young lady. If it's trash talk you want, just you wait." With that he picked up his tennis bag, large enough to house several rackets and at least as large as the pros have, put his arms within the straps, hoisted it onto his back, stooped downward undoubtedly because of extra weight, and shuffled forward looking like Groucho Marx in one of his old movies.

"Randy, I don't know whether to follow you or catch you. Which is it?" All he did was to grunt as he motioned for me to close the door to his office as we marched on.

We arrived at the courts and proceeded to the one he had reserved. He immediately sat down on the bench, opened his bag, pulled out three rackets and selected the one he would use, replaced the others in the bag, pulled out a towel and a bottle of Gatorade, opened two cans of new tennis balls, adjusted his glasses, cinched up Velcro neoprene wraps for his back, each calf and knee, and one elbow, put a sweat band around his forehead, then added a cap with a floppy brim that surrounded his head, rose up, went through several stretches including one for his neck, and finally announced he was good to go. To top everything off, he went through the motions of running in place just like the pros, although I am not sure either foot ever left the ground. Then he looked at me and my astonished grin, and said: "What are you waiting for; let's rumble."

So we went to our respective sides, stood at the baseline, and began to warm up. He was left-handed, spun the ball constantly even when I went to the net for some practice volleys that made it impossible to practice, and never hit the ball directly to me. Nothing had pace. Everything was slow and slower. After no more than five minutes Mann announced, "I am ready anytime."

I replied: "OK, do you wish to spin the racket for serve? Up or down?"

He didn't respond to my questions. Instead, he took all three balls, went to the baseline, and simply announced: "I'm ready, first ball in."

So I yelled back, "Randy, that's not real tennis." And before I was set, his first serve was on its way and slicing into my right hip. He handcuffed me badly and my return did not make it to the net. Game underway.

His strategy was one of find your opponent's weakness and strength, and then play constantly to the former. I thrived on power and had little patience for extended rallies. I preferred coming to the net and hitting winners even if high risk. Mann quickly understood this. He dinked the ball constantly, sliced and diced me back and forth and from side to side, and forced me to hit off balance. Before I knew it, I had made mistake after mistake, had lost four straight games with two at love, and had to change my tactics. But I didn't immediately. My frustration heightened with each game as Mann would bring me up to the net with a drop shot, and then lob my return to the baseline. Before I knew it, the score was six love, and the set was over.

At that point, Mann asked if he could sit down for a moment. The day was warm — about 90 degrees — and he was already drenched with sweat. "I need a break — hope you understand. Surprised you, didn't I. It's called GRIT." And then he unzipped the main compartment to his gigantic tennis bag, searched around, pulled out another Gatorade and opened it, searched around again and finally pulled out a sandwich.

"Randy, what's that?"

"What do you think it is? A sandwich, peanut butter and jelly. Do you want some? I also have turkey and tuna salad somewhere down there."

I couldn't believe it. "Randy, now I know why your bag is so large and stuffed. Can I rummage around your bag, or is it much too dangerous?" Before he could reply, I leaned over and took a quick peek. "My goodness Randy, do I see exam blue books in there?"

He simply replied: "Which year do you wish to see?"

"Professor, we answer exam questions with computers these days. This has to be from the dark ages."

He calmly said: "From not that long ago." And then he reached into his bag, removed a turkey sandwich and a Gatorade from a small cooler within the bag, and handed them to me. So we sat for a while quietly and simply ate and drank. This was his ritual at restaurants with several stars as well as for sandwiches by the side of a steamy tennis court.

When finished, he stood up, retightened each of his six Velcro wraps, did some more stretches including an elaborate one for his neck, and once again ran in place without raising his feet off the ground. Mann then motioned to me as if to say it was time to resume play. And we did, but this time I was ready for him. Mann was visibly tired, maybe even exhausted. A power game was futile because I was too erratic and impatient. But I could also dink and move him around, especially bring him to the net and then move him back to the baseline or maybe drive it right by him. Yet he never gave up or gave in. He tried to run down and retrieve everything all the way to the end of our match. More than anything, he was too tired for a second and third set, which I won 6–2, and 6–2. But he insisted on playing to the end. After exchanging congratulations, we both sat back down on the bench. He reached into his bag and pulled out yet another Gatorade. Mann then opened it, but before taking a swig he said: "Billie, well done. Now that was a demonstration of resilience and resourcefulness. Bravo. You got grit and game. I guess sports yield transcendent messages for everything, even law school and certainly for life."

"Randy, I thought, and clearly hoped, that all we were doing was hitting a ball back and forth, without serious messages, in a game called tennis."

With that Mann went silent for a while as he enjoyed his cool drink and cooled down. And then he said: "Billie, just one thing."

"Randy, not that again!"

"No, I just need a ride home. We have one car and my wife needed it today, so she dropped me off at school hoping you could bring me back. It's not far, and I believe it's on your way."

"No problem, I would be happy to Randy. When do you wish to leave?"

"How about now."

So we both climbed into my Smart Car—with no place for his tennis bag other than his lap—and headed to the Western edge of College City where he and his wife lived in a three bedroom condo. Climbing up and out of the car required my help because of tight quarters and a stiffened back. After making it to the sidewalk with my continued assistance, Mann hoisted his tennis bag onto his back, straightened up, motioned for me to follow, and barked back at me: "No helping me in front of my wife!" We then entered the building and trudged up to the second floor. Bending over with the weight of the bag causing him to sway, Mann searched for his key among his pockets, found it, unlocked the door, turned the handle, entered the dining room/living room to 201, and shouted: "Berke, I'm home safe and sound."

Sitting on a couch, reading a book and directly ahead, was Berke, Mann's wife. "Randy, no need to shout; I'm right here. So tell me, what did you injure today? Anything strained, torn, or broken? Any immediate trip to the Emergency Room?" And then she saw me. "Who are you, may I ask?"

"I am Billie Williams, Professor Mann's research assistant this summer, also his tennis opponent for the day."

"Well did you let him win?"

"No way did I, or would I!"

"Good—because he always wants to win and I mean badly."

"I know that feeling," I said softly, perhaps not loud enough for her to hear. Meanwhile, Mann excused himself to unwrap himself and put some things away, but certainly not to empty his tennis bag of all things concealed.

Berke then got up from the couch, rearranged her glasses, and approached me with the erect posture of a marine. I immediately noticed how short she was, well under five feet and probably never close to it. I had imagined Mann as once over six feet, perhaps well over. And I visualized wedding photos, including the first dance with Berke looking up and up. And then she spoke, this time with the authority of a marine sergeant. "My, you are young, younger than I thought. What can I get you to eat? You must be hungry."

"Mrs. Mann, actually not, the Professor shared his sandwiches and other goodies, and he had lots to share. Do I have you to thank for that?"

"Actually not. Randy is responsible for his own breakfast and lunch. I take responsibility for his nightly sumptuous suppers. Now then, how about some dessert? Do you have a sweet tooth?"

"Yes, and yes," I replied.

We went into the kitchen, which was spotless and carefully arranged for aesthetics and efficiency. Berke sat me at the kitchen table, offered me some iced coffee, and immediately passed a plateful of cookies. Afterwards, she removed from the refrigerator a plateful of toffee and put it down on the table. And finally she warmed a coffee cake, and when properly heated, she added it to the sweets to be eaten, or at least tasted, while informing me that all three of the sweets were homemade with the latter derived from a secret family recipe. At once I began to eat from all three selections, and at this point Mann entered the room. Berke immediately observed my pleasure, while Mann seemed focused on Berke's pleasure. He also remained silent as his wife took over the conversation wanting to know everything about me while leaving me little opportunity to respond. Nevertheless, she was satisfied enough to like me, I think, because she removed from the refrigerator more cookies, toffee, and cake, put them in a container, and then announced that she was preparing a "care package" to go. After a while longer, I told her it was time for me to leave, and then I thanked her for the goodies and the Professor for the tennis. With the "care package" in hand, Berke gave me a warm hug and told me that henceforth I was on their permanent invitation list for celebrations of holidays with family and friends, and that I would be hearing from her. And I did the following Thanksgiving. But I declined. To this day, I am not sure why. Perhaps I was still uncomfortable with Mann, his lectures about life, and the prospect of close friendship.

The following week Mann presented me a manuscript he had finally completed that utilized the research I had done for him over the summer, and I immediately noticed — but never anticipated — an acknowledgement on the cover page. Mann then asked me to read this draft carefully, and make some notes on anything and everything that came to mind, including organization, theses, arguments, and prose. And he wanted me ready to discuss this in one week. I was overwhelmed by the magnitude of the task but even more so by the respect and apparent trust evidenced by both the assignment and the acknowledgement. It took me two days to read and reread the manuscript carefully and another to simply give it thought. It was easy to edit his prose. I had had lots of experience doing that in my two years in public relations before law school, and Mann's style was too often convoluted, dominated by the passive voice, and surprisingly punctuated. That alone would give me a lot to notate and discuss, but I wanted something more, something organizational, global, or analytical. Something that went to the heart of his ideas and would knock his socks off. I wanted to impress with something he knew improved the piece significantly. But little came to me, and what did surface left me on thin ice with written comments destined to be dismissed. After one week I was prepared but not ready.

"OK, Billie what do you have?"

I immediately handed him a ten page memo that began with the edits — which also appeared on the manuscript itself — and concluded with just one page on the ideas and structural organization that underscored his piece. He scanned the entire ten pages and then carefully read the last. Finally, Mann looked up and simply said: "Billie, well done. Let's go through everything you have noted and suggested. Let's do it one comment at a time. I forewarn you, this conference may last more than a day, but it will give me an opportunity to talk through and think through everything you have had to say. Are you good to go?" Mann didn't wait for a response, but immediately continued "let's begin with your final observations on the last page." After rereading the last page again, Mann said: "Billie your observations are self-explanatory, precisely targeted, important, and worthy of careful consideration. And I must do exactly that, but I need further time for careful thought."

"Professor, are you trying to say that you require a long lunch in solitude, with good food and peace and quiet?"

"Exactly, Billie, you already know me much too well." Two days later he called me into his office to review my last page of comments and carefully explained his reasoning for rejecting each one; but in doing so, Mann confirmed the worth and serious attention he attached to my ideas. This was his greatest compliment of all.

Next, we began to review my edits one-by-one and page-by-page. He had no objections to greater clarity and brevity achieved through consistent use of the active voice. Nor did he object to clarity achieved through shifting the position and order of sentences and even paragraphs. Mann consistently would ask for my explanation, think for a moment or more, and then simply reply with a firmly stated YES. But punctuation was another matter. We stalled with each recommendation.

"Professor, you must insert a comma between these two clauses."

"Billie, no."

"Why, no? A comma is required. Didn't you ever diagram sentences in grade school and discover where commas belonged?"

"Billie, I did, but my answer remains NO!"

"Professor, but why?"

"Because I hadn't run out of breath at the end of that clause. It doesn't satisfy the BREATH TEST."

"What did you say? The BREATH TEST!"

"You heard me."

"Professor, it makes no sense. What kind of breath, deep, shallow or what, and whose breath?"

"Billie, the author, of course, who must breathe normally in punctuating each sentence."

"Professor, we each breathe differently just as we read and speak at different speeds. The punctuation for commas is sure to be different for a person from Dixie with COPD than a marathoner from New York City. Shouldn't rules for punctuation be designed to yield consistency?" But he stuck to his guns, giving in some of the time, and insisted that the BREATH TEST prevail.

Afterwards I asked: "The BREATH TEST, where did it come from?"

"My mother."

"You have a mother?"

"Yes, Billie, I have a mother or had. Don't we all have mothers; unless you believe I descended from another planet much like Superman. And even he had a mother, actually two. My mother also intensely disapproved of beer signs."

"Beer signs? What are beer signs? I haven't seen that terminology in blue books, white books, or any book on grammar or effective writing."

"A beer sign uses markers and punctuation as a substitute for words to achieve emphasis or explanation. You know—things like repeated underlining or quotation marks to highlight a phrase or expression. Or the use of endless quotations from the work of others as a substitute for an author's own effort at clear explanation or summary."

"Professor, beer signs? But why did she call them beer signs?"

"I have no idea. Except—I do recall as a kid how much she despised signs that cluttered country highways, especially signs for beer and Burma Shave. I guess she was an early environmentalist when it came to protecting the beauty of rural America from the invasion of commercialism."

"Was your mother a school teacher who trumped your own?"

"No, Billie, she was a practicing lawyer. Yes, Billie, a practicing lawyer who graduated from law school in the year I was born."

I did a quick calculation and said: "She must have graduated in the late 1920s. Was she the only woman in her class?"

"Yes, Billie, and she graduated at the top much to the disappointment, even hostility, of classmates. But there were no jobs for women anywhere in private practice with large firms, but there was a job waiting for her as a secretary."

"Did she accept it?"

"Yes, it was with a prestigious firm with prestigious lawyers who never acknowledged her law degree or brilliance or dared ask 'what do you think?' My parents were poor and early signs of the Great Depression were rearing their head. Quite simply, they had to have work, and that was the closest she could get to the law."

"What did your father do?"

"My parents were married in 1926. My father had just gotten a Masters in Architecture. He worked as a draftsman for several years, but when the Depression arrived full bore, jobs for architects and even draftsmen became nonexistent. After that, he was a day laborer sometimes and jobless most of the time. We lived with my uncle and grandmother who basically raised me until I was ready for school. But by then, my father's heart was broken, and he simply gave up and gave in to becoming an original 'house mom.' He was good at that, no, I should say great, and also writing poetry and children's stories. He took over at the same time my mother left her secretarial job and opened her own office. And they did not starve. My mother worked 'day and night,' her favorite expression and also the reason why I remained an only child, and she soon succeeded. She accepted every kind of law work imaginable and pleased and kept her clients, and within ten years, she had created her own small firm that lasted until the day she retired. She was an outstanding lawyer and an even better rainmaker. My mother taught me about hard work, dedication, and success, especially how to achieve it but not how to enjoy it. And she also taught me about duty and being dutiful and the leverage achieved through selective guilt."

"And what did your father teach you?"

"My father—he gave me a love for sports and playing them, but most of all, he taught me about life, especially appreciation of music, laughter, good books, and the infinite value of friendships. That's it in a nutshell, and a nutshell is all you get."

"Professor, I have another question."

"Billie, just one more, I have already shared too much. You must do as I say and not as I do, just one more!"

"What does the initial 'E' stand for?"

"Ellsworth."

"Ellsworth?"

"That's what I said!"

"Where did that come from?"

"Billie, it reflects heritage or perhaps a desire to hide it, not the heritage you might imagine. It isn't a family name. Mann is a creation of Ellis Island, and Ellsworth and Randall are attempts at assimilation."

"So why don't you call yourself Ellsworth?"

"Because I hate the name. Just imagine, standing on the mound or at the free throw line and having to contend with 'Elly-Nelly, Nelly-Elly.' It's humiliating when you're eight, perhaps motivating when you're 16. But add to that, I like Randy much better. Elly worked for Elston Howard, but he was bigger than I was and also legendary."

"Professor, I would never have guessed; quite frankly, I like the name Ellsworth."

"Billie, heritage can be consuming, both the good and the bad. But enough is enough. I believe law professors should be one part brilliant and one part mysterious, and with this discussion I breached my commitment to the latter." And with that, our editing work session abruptly concluded.

Soon the summer was coming to an end, the beginning of school was two weeks away, and my work was nearly over with just a few things left to complete. Mann wanted one more lunch together, just the two of us. We went back to his favorite Italian restaurant and enjoyed a very good meal mostly in silence. No more questions, big or small. No more lectures, practical or profound. And no more introductions with "just one more question" or "just one more thing." Most of all, I detected sadness in his eyes and demeanor. No tears, just sadness. Mann had written in one of his articles that graduations for him were always a time of sadness. People he liked and sometimes loved were passing out of his life. It was inevitable. I never asked him whether he felt the same way about research assistants, but he must have. Mann also shared with me that in dialoguing with students in class, he always zeroed in on the eyes of students. Their eyes told him everything he needed to know — confidence, fear, panic, hostility, comprehension, and certainly confusion. Mann's eyes had reddened and I knew everything I needed to know. As we were getting ready to leave, Mann said: "Billie, you did well. Your work was excellent and I enjoyed having you as my RA. If you need any letters of recommendation or help in landing a job or clerkship, just let me know."

All I could manage to say was "thank you very much!" And then I surprised him — and myself — by initiating a big hug in which we never seemed to let go. And that was that, my summer experience with E. Randall Mann.

P.S. Well I remained in law school, redirected myself and some of my habits for preparation — particularly exams — and I improved upon my second semester performance throughout my second and third years of school. And I really did well, not top one or two percent, but top ten, and with it the Order of Coif, law school's version of Phi Beta Kappa. Then came a U.S. District Court clerkship for one year with a former student of Mann (his letter of recommendation didn't hurt). The next year I took a job with the litigation department of a large prestigious firm in Minneapolis. But I didn't like it. The next year, I moved to a medium sized litigation firm also in Minneapolis. And I disliked it even more. Two years later, I opened my own office there and concentrated on family law. I had no exposure to the subject until my last year of school when I took the basic course from my criminal law teacher, who had been my favorite throughout school. And she didn't disappoint. So I took another elective in the area but never thought of pursuing it professionally. Yet ultimately, I took a chance, opened an office, and shared space with one of the best divorce lawyers, who helped me with all I needed to know.

I soon discovered that I was very good at it. I really surprised myself too. It wasn't the competition and the taste for victory that motivated me or made me excel, it was something quite different. I was good at many things that came naturally. I was very good with clients in distress. I could gain their trust and complete confidence. Yes, they liked me and my judgment. Additionally, I could easily see and frame the big picture. What was possible, what was likely, and where inevitably we would end up. I could negotiate with calm and a positive attitude that seemed to blunt the sharp edges of the other side and maintain civility. And judges liked and respected me because I was straightforward, no nonsense, and never wasted the court's time, especially with meaningless and time consuming petitions and motions. Bottom line, I could achieve excellent results, not necessarily victories. The process of divorce seldom yields singular victories, certainly when children and custody are involved. Things are almost never black and white, always shades of grey that seem to justify the position and feelings of both parties, especially when you hear their side individually. Perhaps the best part thus far, my clients don't come through their divorce with anything but praise for me. In fact they give me other business. I get their wills, their trusts, and, at this point, the estates of parents, and I help them when they buy or sell their homes. Yes, I do family law, but even more, I AM A FAMILY LAWYER. I work very hard, prepare better than anyone, and deep-down know each day that I do good work and am a good lawyer.

I also have a life beyond work. I am married to a non-lawyer with no children, at least not yet. I still play competitive basketball, still point guard, still good at it, but mainly in men's adult leagues.

My life as a law student, lawyer, and even a person has not been a failure as I once projected and cried out to Mann. Have I thought of him often? I do like long lunches, by myself, while experiencing the joys of good food and resolving the problems of the day in peace and quiet. But does Mann surface in conscious thought, NO, not even the sermons he once laid on me. At least not until now as I give this account eight years later. After ending my summer position with Mann, we would see each other occasionally at school. Our greetings would be brief and formal. No more lunches and no more confidences. And after graduation, no more contact. But at graduation, following the ceremony, he searched for me and found me with my parents. He congratulated them first, and then he looked at me directly and said: "Billie, you rediscovered your GRIT — TRUE GRIT — I have the utmost respect for TRUE GRIT. I am so proud of you. Billie, one more thing — have a great life, you are really capable of that!" I replied "thanks" almost inaudibly, and then he smiled at me and my parents and was on his way. And that was that.

As I said, after graduation, no more contact. I could have written or called or visited when in town. But I didn't. I could have shared with him news of the life I had made and loved both professionally and beyond. But I didn't. I could have and should have. Because with his recent death, that opportunity is forever lost. Did he ever learn what became of me? I do not know. Someone must have told him even though no one probably remembered the summer I worked for him. Someone, perhaps, but none of my classmates were among his students and, because of his retirement years earlier, I am certain most of my classmates didn't know he ever existed. Mann once said to me that the institutional memory of current students never exceeds three years — a simple fact of life — and for faculty colleagues, it's not much longer. And during my time, his retirement was more than ten years before. Yet no matter, Mann knew me too well, I think better than I knew myself. He did say he was proud of me; he must have known that I would continue to make him proud. With that I must live. That's all I have.

CHAPTER 2

THE BEST TEACHER I HAVE EVER KNOWN: MR. BB

E. Randall Mann

I loved my mother and, as a child, Saturdays and sometimes Sundays were my time with her. She was the breadwinner of the family, at first because the Great Depression had destroyed all professional opportunities for my father, who was an architect by education and training, and later all ambition and hope, as even jobs as a draftsman and later a day laborer evaporated. But the Depression never spiraled into personal depression as he became a great Mr. Mom at home and an even better father. My grandmother lived with us and raised me at home until about age five, and after that my father did. But Saturday was their day off, and my mother viewed it as a time for bonding. A day at her office was our special time together.

I admired my mother and wanted to be like her. Not because she was a brilliant and respected lawyer. But because she (and my father as well) were tall, actually close to six feet two inches. And I wanted to be taller, or at least as tall, mainly because of sports. Specifically, basketball. But they were also thin, painfully thin, and I did not want to be thin, which I was. I wanted to be big horizontally as well a vertically. Because of football. I could not work at vertical, but I could at horizontal. And so I ate and I ate. My mother would send me on foot to the local bakery for one loaf of to-die-for out-of-the-oven rye bread, which I would bring home half devoured. Soon she adjusted with an order for two loaves which always transitioned into one when I came through the door, and still she greeted me with a smile and stifled laughter.

My mother was brilliant, first in her class at law school, also the only woman in school for all of her three years, and jobless at graduation in 1930. All the large firms welcomed her as a valued secretary but none as a licensed lawyer. So after graduation she set up shop on her own, working mainly from our cramped apartment while she tried everything to get permanent employment somewhere. Over time working for others became less attractive, and within a few years she discovered her abilities as a rainmaker and became determined to build her own firm. Bernard Berenz was two years behind my mother in school and matched her brilliance and record. The toll of the Great Depression upon businesses and law firms had gotten worse; there were no jobs, especially for recent graduates. And if the prospects for starvation working alone seemed inevitable, why not risk it as partners?

Looking back, it seems as if I had known Bernard Berenz forever. Though I am told it was age four, my recollections begin a bit later. As I said, Saturdays were my time with my mother, but they soon became special times WITH "Mr. BB." I couldn't easily pronounce Berenz at first, and so it morphed into Mr. BB. And it stuck until the time of his death at age ninety-five. I always had to call him Mr. BB, even after I became a lawyer and worked for him, just the two of us and also with others. I never could address him by his first name. He asked me to call him Bernie, which was warm and personal. But Mr. was out of respect, and he had earned more respect than anyone I knew.

My first impressions of Mr. BB, at least those I could really recall, were austere. He was after all of serious purpose, but when he smiled and revealed his dimpled chin, he was instantly transformed into warmth and comfort. Mr. BB seemed always behind his desk at work, in a white shirt with a tie and rolled up sleeves (even though it was Saturday and sometimes Sunday, with no prospect of a client walking through the front door), with his head down reading or writing in longhand, or looking out through his office window in deep solitary thought working through the nitty gritty of problems under his care. Occasionally, he would rise and pace while carefully thinking through and analyzing every issue before him. Now and then he would see me through his open door seated at a table in the office library tracing comic book characters with onion skin paper provided by my mother or reading the latest Hardy boy mystery. Before me was a single six ounce bottle of Coca Cola rationed by my mother from the small refrigerator kept in a closet to be nursed throughout our day together at the office. As my impatience mounted over several hours (and my Coca Cola became a casualty to poor planning), I would get up, walk around, and quietly peek into his office. Although his back might be facing the door, he would always turn and deliver a broad and friendly smile. I was certain that he had the powers of Superman and maybe even more—super hearing and eyes in the back of his head. At first, all he could coax out of me was "Hi Mr. BB," nothing more.

After several of these brief doorway stopovers, Mr. BB asked me what I was reading. I quickly showed him the Hardy boy book that my mother had purchased several hours earlier which I was determined to finish by nightfall. After several questions about whether I liked to read that I impatiently answered, he smiled once again as if to release me from interrogation and my unease. But the following Saturday, he had a gift for me when I peeked in for a stopover, actually two gifts, copies of *The Adventures of Tom Sawyer* and *The Iron Duke*. He said I might be too young for either, but try them. Which I did. And so it was each week with something new added to my reading to interest me, to challenge me, to broaden my horizon, and, with it all, to experience the joy of learning. Next came word games that began with lists for me to create. Synonyms. Antonyms. Homonyms. After that, numbers and math that were pure fun. Mr. BB gave me newspaper assignments from the sports section that involved batting averages, earned run averages, slugging percentages, and games out of first place. Much later came front section news and editorials which didn't seem like fun, at least not at first, because I didn't realize that he was teaching me about forming my own opinions as well as the components of sound and effective argumentation. I also discovered something else; Mr. BB sometimes stammered and stuttered, especially when forming and explaining complex thoughts with great care, precision, and clarity. It never bothered me. Nor did it bother clients, especially after they came to appreciate fully what Mr. BB finally had to say, always a giant benefit to patient listening.

There were also rewards. Foremost were Mr. BB's smile and laughter, especially when I surprised him with something he didn't anticipate. But there were things tangible as well that are among my earliest recollections. Trips down to the street level of the office building and then next door to Walgreens to sit at a counter and have lunch together. He liked a tuna sandwich best and almost always ordered it along with coffee. For me, it was a hamburger, nothing on it, french fries, and a chocolate milkshake. The latter was the best part. It came with a large glass that was always filled to the brim with whip cream and a cherry on top. Along with it also came the metal container in which the shake was made, still half full and ice cold. Finally, a cellophane package with two delicious cookies. The shake and cookies were my favorite part and I always made the most of both by nursing them through to the end of, and sometimes beyond, the time Mr. BB could allocate to lunch.

My mother never realized that Mr. BB and I would disappear weekly for lunch at Walgreens. She was much too busy with work and occasional clients with Saturday appointments. This presented no problem until she recognized that something was on a collision course with another Saturday ritual she had created for just her and her son, a mid-afternoon lunch on our trip home. At the end of the EL-line and bus stop that followed was her favorite delicatessen, Bennies on Bryn Mawr. She loved everything they made, especially their chopped liver and corned beef. It was within walking distance of home and was a long-standing family hangout for supper. One Saturday, she expressed her concern: "Ellie, are you feeling OK, maybe I should take you to see Dr. Stern?"

"Mom, why are you asking?"

"Ellie, because each week you have less and less for lunch, and you must be very hungry by three o'clock."

"No, Mom I'm fine!"

The following week I shared this conversation with Mr. BB, and he advised me to spill the beans. He also told me that he never wished to interfere with a mother-son lunch and that from now on our trips to Walgreens would only be on Saturdays in which my mother couldn't have lunch with me. I was very unhappy about this. Bennies may have had the best chopped liver and corned beef, but their milkshakes were never accompanied by the metal container or the two cookies.

By the time I reached age seven, or maybe it was eight, I was introduced to the violin, and with it came mandatory lessons — as well as daily practice — with a teacher whose studio was downtown near my mother's office. The violin had been an essential component of the history of both my mother's and father's family. The violin experience had to be passed on to each generation, partly because of love of music but mainly because it had been a way out of the ghetto even if for the gifted only. Yet I was not among them. Nevertheless, after each lesson, when I arrived at the office and did my stop-over in Mr. BB's doorway, he would ask me to play for him. Which I did. And he listened patiently and intently to tunes faintly resembling pieces he had known, always accompanied by screeches that made them undiscernible. Although his expression said differently, Mr. BB always offered a measure of praise. And with that praise came mention of recordings of famous violin concertos performed by famous violinists and occasionally gifts of the recordings themselves at 78rpms. Everything was a learning experience. The violin remained a part of my life, and Mr. BB's, until I was thirteen and my parents asked me whether I wanted to continue lessons. Without hesitation I said NO.

And they replied, "Really? That isn't the answer we expected. Don't make a choice you'll soon regret. Now then, what do you wish to do?"

"Not continue," I said.

"You'll regret it!"

But I didn't, not for a moment, especially after I discovered brass instruments to play in high school. Nor did Mr. BB regret my choice as to play or not to play.

About age twelve, Mr. BB escalated my learning curve, first with books and ultimately with words. To this day I can hear his voice when he had something very important to say. It would always begin with "Ellie," the nickname people had given me. The initial "E." that I have been using for my adult life is short for Ellsworth, a product of immigrant assimilation. My mother and father preferred Ellsworth and that's what they usually called me. I hated both Ellsworth and the friendly substitute, Ellie. Too much like a girl. Later in life I became Randy, short for Randall, my middle name. And it stuck. But Mr. BB liked Ellie, and because he was who he was, I never said otherwise or even hinted at something different.

"Ellie, I have several things for you to read over time, probably years to come. A book of Shakespeare plays and another containing his sonnets. I urge you to read them and over the years to reread them. Human connection may not begin with words, but ultimately it depends upon them. What we say, and how we say it, shapes our existence within family, community, country, and the world. Words are like the finest of jewels, to be valued and treasured. They can cause joy, pain, sorrow; indeed all human emotions. They convey ideas big and small, complex and simple, and dangerous and secure. They can function like a scalpel or sledge hammer, or a sword or shield. They can reflect compassion, love, anger, hostility, and all things good and bad. Ellie, you must learn to use them, to command them, and to make them work effectively for you. And further, you must recognize that one never fully understands something or develops an idea of importance until one can express and explain it. In short, command of language is the centerpiece of all clear analysis. One cannot think clearly without the ability to write clearly. So, let's get started."

And get started we did, step-by-step, baby ones at first, and giant ones within a few years. To begin with, he would ask me to select something from the newspaper. Anything, front section, sports section, editorial page, opinion page. And we would both read it carefully. He would ask a question, and then I could choose a question. Simple or profound question, it didn't matter. And then we would write an answer to both of our questions. After that, we would do the same with chapters taken from my textbooks at school. And from there, we progressed to some poetry, magazine articles, and short stories that interested me. What did I like and what didn't I like? And then tell him why in writing. And progress we did. By the time I reached high school, Mr. BB was giving me some opinions from the U.S. Supreme Court to read. "Ellie, which opinions appeal to you?"

"But Mr. BB, I am unfamiliar with the law that applies; I can't come up with something sensible."

And so he gave me a copy of the U.S. Constitution. "Ellie, let's start with this. What do you understand it to say?" Above all, Mr. BB had extraordinary confidence in the capacity of courts to achieve results that made sense. And if an argument, proposition, or decision did not, its life expectancy would not be lasting.

These exercises continued until I entered high school and found girls, concert band, and varsity sports, and they also coincided with his need to parent his own three children, five years old and younger, and so my Saturday stop-overs with Mr. BB came to a screeching halt. These memories that I recount were life altering and, without more, would have been enough for an entire lifetime and establish Mr. BB as a treasured friend and the best teacher I have ever known.

High school came and went, and then I was off to an Ivy League college. I majored in political science expecting I might like to teach, but my mother would have none of that. She saw my future with her, mother and son working together while she prepared me to take over the business she had created, grown, and carefully cultivated. She would say to me again and again: "This business I have built is for you, no one else. Why do you think I have worked night and day? It is for you my son and only child! It is your destiny and duty." Over the summer I wanted to remain on the East Coast and work, but again she would have none of that. "I want you in my office working at least part time, so I can get you a head start on law school and the profession." And so I did exactly that. I was an only child but never indulged like one. I was other-directed by both parents to satisfy their needs, aspirations, and even moods, and their principal tool for accomplishing this was guilt. Huge and constant doses of straightforward guilt that sometimes worked with a blink of an eye, a heavy sigh, or two simple phrases—"never mind" or "I'll do it myself."

The work those summers, even though part time, was awful. Mainly I followed her around and watched her try cases, which always settled before I could learn anything, and also meet with clients to solve business problems I did not understand and plan the estates of clients young and old. One thing I did learn is that my mother was very good at saying all the things clients wanted to hear, at least about themselves. She was a natural and expert at flattery. That bothered me, because it always was too much and too broad and always smelled like bullshit. The clients apparently loved it, but it was something I knew immediately I could not do, or wanted to do, when it was my turn to step into the role my mother would carve out for me: her replacement as rainmaker. My mother also wanted me to learn something about law and law books. That training amounted to inserting supplements, page by page, into treatises. This was a task I could have done and might have enjoyed with a sense of self-importance ten years earlier. I did, however, get to see Mr. BB and have occasional lunches with him. Always at Walgreens; tuna and hamburger, coffee, milkshake, and two cookies. Again, there were always gentle questions in which he would probe things I was learning, enjoying, and interested in; yet at the same time, he always stayed away from the subject of law school and a future at their law firm.

Then came graduation from college summa cum laude. My parents were proud and tearful, both had night school college educations, but their son was Ivy League with honors to certify their dreams and aspirations. By then I had given up on my own destiny and given in to theirs. I had been accepted by another Ivy League law school and enrolled the following fall with full support from my parents, both financial and moral. That summer, I rented a small apartment near school, got a job with a friend's family business, and met a terrific woman who had also just graduated from college. Berke was everything I had hoped for, and I knew early on that I wanted to marry her. And we did five years later.

Law school was much more difficult than anything I had ever encountered or anticipated. I was surrounded by the best of the best among the students and the faculty. The readings were difficult and could be read, understood, and analyzed at a pace matched only by snails. The faculty asked questions that always raised more questions, uncertainty, and confusion. And they orchestrated dialogues that pushed each of us to our limits. My head ached every day. Yet I felt invigorated and excited by the challenges presented by law school and the opportunities that stood in the wings with a professional lifetime yet to come. Despite confusion, uncertainty, and wonderment about whether I would ever be prepared to take a final exam, I felt assured by past academic success and the arrogance that was part of my elite college experience. In short, I felt superior. And before my first set of final exams, I had grades on papers in the legal writing and research course to back it up. Yet I was wrong.

First semester grades were posted not long after the second semester began. One B-, two B's, and one C+. No A's! How did this happen? It never had before! I was stunned, unhappy, and disgruntled, not ready to pack it in, but contemplating how I would do better at a second level law school back home. Yet I never mentioned transferring to anyone. I called home the following weekend, and in response to "what's new," I answered, "prepare yourselves for mediocrity," and then explained. They never could or would accept mediocrity for their son whose future was destined to enhance their future and even their present. They said several things trying to cheer me up, and then said goodbye. When I hung up, I was surprised that it was among the shortest phone conversations of the school year.

Within a few days, I received a call from Mr. BB. It was our first since I had begun law school. Although I welcomed it, I was surprised, until he shared that my parents had called and asked him to contact me. We discussed a number of things about law school life and then got down to the subject of my exams. Mr. BB then asked me whether I had seen my exam papers and discussed them with respective teachers. I had not. Then he asked me if I had carbon copies of my legal writing papers. I did. And would I immediately mail them to him? I did. I immediately posted them and then waited impatiently for his response.

One week later I heard from Mr. BB by phone. The call lasted over two hours, much longer that any long distance call I had known. Given the year, it must have cost a fortune, or so it seemed. Mr. BB took over the conversation from beginning to end making it almost a monologue. "OK, Ellie, I want to review each of these papers with you." And he did, one-by-one, both globally and even paragraph-by-paragraph. He focused on the research, the analysis, and prose. His suggestions seemed minor, but his praise was major. "Ellie, you are good, very good. Your work is exceptional. Now know this: you will do well in law school, maybe not as well as you expect, but you will do well. Even more important, you will be an outstanding lawyer. Quite frankly, these memoranda are worthy of the best and most experienced associates I have known. Now then, do you wish to do better on your exams?"

"Mr. BB, yes, of course!"

"Ellie, then here is what I recommend. See each of your teachers and ask to review your exam papers. Whether or not they focus on what I mention, I want you to look for this telltale problem. Most legal problems present core issues from which secondary issues are generated. In a sense, the core issue can be likened to the trunk of a tree. I am confident that you found and focused on core issues and that you analyzed them and resolved them by reaching a result or by pursuing a single branch of the tree and identifying a secondary issue. But I also expect that you ignored branches that took you in different directions. Those branches may not have reflected the probable resolution of the core issue, but they were defensible and plausible, and they should, time permitting, always be identified and discussed. To put it differently, at every crossroad, I suspect you headed in one direction only. Superior legal analysis requires one to acknowledge and even pursue the other direction or directions that might lead to additional important issues. And on an exam, one should at least mention them even when pressed for time. In short, you have to see more branches of the tree and where they might lead so long as there is a plausible basis for each. Ellie, I suspect this is the source of your problem, and with this adjustment, you will improve significantly on your exams."

"Mr. BB, why do you say this?"

"Ellie, you forget. With all the time we have spent together, I KNOW how you think."

I knew he knew me well, but I never thought anyone could know me that well. Yet I trusted his judgment and was determined to do better. So I visited each of my teachers, read my examination answers carefully, and discovered important tree branches that I neither mentioned nor explored. Mr. BB was right. I was humbled and very appreciative and wrote him a long letter expressing both. And with that knowledge I got immediate results. By graduation, my transcript was dominated by A's and I rose to the top five percent of my class. As I recount this experience many years later and examine Mr. BB's praise of my legal writing papers and his advice about exams and legal analysis,

I now clearly recognize that his praise was an overstatement and his advice an understatement. The first to support and uplift me. The second to give me strong direction—his first dose of criticism, albeit constructive.

During my last year of law school, my mother visited me to discuss my future. "Ellie, you may wish to apply for a judicial clerkship. That would be fine with me. You may also wish to go work for one of the large firms for a few years and let them train you and shape you into a real lawyer. That would be OK with me. But I know what's good for you and what you'll ultimately want for yourself; to come back and take over my practice in time. It's your destiny." MY DES-TINY! I had no choice. It was not a bad choice; it was a good choice. Still I had no choice. So I made the decision to begin my professional life with Mann and Berenz and leave my training in the good and preferred hands of Mr. BB.

For a while my mother wanted me by her side, just the same as she had while I worked at her firm part time over previous summers. But now she would introduce me to each client as a lawyer who would be working with her, have me take notes, and assign me follow-up tasks drafting research memo-randa, documents, and even appellate briefs. And before showing them to her, have Mr. BB look at my work products. These experiences with my mother gave me full appreciation of many things, foremost was her ability to grasp a problem quickly and to formulate a solution or strategy that addressed legal, business, and often family issues. I had known she was smart, but now I saw her true brilliance and why so many clients wanted HER, a woman, as their lawyer in all things that mattered. It wasn't the less than credible schmoozing I had witnessed earlier; it was her ability to navigate a client successfully through all kinds of problems big and small. I could never understand this until I became a lawyer and could appreciate the magnitude of what she was accomplishing for clients and for herself. She wasn't just a good lawyer; my mother was a great lawyer.

One evening, I stayed late at the office; eventually, it became very late. While searching for a particular file, I stumbled upon work my mother had done be-fore partnering with Mr. BB for one of her original clients in her earliest years of practice. The file included internal memos summarizing relevant law and its application to the problem, letters to the client summarizing the problem and outlining strategies for success, and trial and appellate briefs. And I read everything carefully. Once again, there was affirmation of greatness. She could make rain with the best, but she could also match the skill-set and work prod-ucts of elite craftsmen anywhere. The following Friday night, I joined my parents for supper as I did most Friday nights. And I revealed my joy in discovering something from her professional past. "Mom, you are a great lawyer. I would be exceedingly pleased to ever author work products of that high quality." She smiled and began to change the subject. But I wouldn't let her. "Mom, talk to me. Instead of 'advance sheets' to file over college summers, why didn't you give me your written work to read?" Again, she changed the subject. "Mom, but I need an answer. Why did you give me to Mr. BB for training instead of you?"

Finally, she addressed my question. "Ellie, I leaned on you hard and long enough. I pushed you to do what I wanted. And when you did, I had second thoughts. My dream was becoming reality, and I didn't want to mess it up. I wanted you to be the best. And the fact is, Bernie is a far better teacher than I. I have known about you and Bernie and your special relationship from the outset, and I was neither displeased or jealous. He has been your mentor throughout, including coming to your rescue in law school. I wanted to give you space along with the best teacher I have ever known. Simple as that." Simple as that, so I left it at that.

From the outset, I was challenged by the diverse tasks, seldom seeing the same kind of transaction or litigation twice. And I was overwhelmed most of all by what I didn't know daily and by the multitasking that required me to juggle twenty assignments simultaneously. I lived in a constant state of ignorance and angst. I liked the work, but not what it did to my psyche until Mr. BB came to my rescue. He had seen me working late every day. Mr. BB caught the 7:15 commuter train home most evenings while I was still there, often until 9 and beyond. One evening as he was about to leave, he asked me how late was I working and whether I was having many problems. He liked the work products I had given him for review, but was there anything I wished to discuss. I said yes, there were problems, and yes, I would like to discuss them. He then told me to come into his office, and we began the first of many extended discussions over the next two years that caused him to miss the 7:15 to Lakeside, and the next, and the next as well. As I mentioned earlier, by then Mr. BB was married and heavily involved with his own children. I knew there was a cost to the time he spent with me and the promises he had to break at home. But he never said anything. I also knew he enjoyed these opportunities to teach just the same as I did to learn.

I began by telling him about my constant state of ignorance and the stress that accompanied it. I explained that with each assignment came a new experience and a steep learning curve. And with twenty things to address at once, I could never do enough to feel confident that I had done enough. This was the way I felt in law school with four or five courses at a time, but now it was much worse. What I did really counted. Lives and livelihoods were at stake, and what I did not do might have serious consequences for others! "Mr. BB, did you ever feel this way?" His response was to smile and burst into reflexive laughter almost as if he enjoyed what I said.

"Ellie, please forgive the laughter, it simply happened. To begin with, I felt the same as you do for ten to fifteen years after law school. I know it's painful, but over time it will subside. But not completely; you never want that. And I would have never wanted it to be different for myself or for you. It's part of becoming an outstanding lawyer, especially in a general practice. Ellie, it's your conscience and strong sense of responsibility at work, and I would never want to be around any lawyer without it. It reflects a desire to do your best at a point in life in which it's difficult to define and accept what is your best. That comes with time, which I'll explain in a moment. But for now you must live with the livable and know it will improve. Ellie, the best criminal defense lawyer I have ever known vomits daily during each of his death penalty trials. Daily! That's the extreme. At the other end of the spectrum is total confidence that might border on arrogance, something my friend fears more than trips to the washroom to relieve nausea. The lawyer I want to hire, or the one I want to represent me, is always the one who asks the question: 'Do I have everything covered?' Especially, the one who has done everything but is still uneasy with his answer.

"Ellie, the angst that accompanies this expression of conscience and sense of responsibility is a huge burden, but, as I said, it will diminish to the point in which, although there, it will be on the back burner. Trust me, it will get better. After all, you have no choice if you wish to be a real lawyer. You can't literally work night and day. You must sustain and nourish yourself with all the things that make you a whole person, and that means a sensible life beyond work. It's a matter of survival. But there is something more that happens that enables you to end your day at the office each evening and set limits for the weekend. To begin with, it rests with experience and learning because you begin to repeat certain kinds of transactions and litigation. The knowledge derived from experience is always an antidote to this species of uncertainty. But more important, there is something powerful that promotes confidence, and it begins with the powers of critical analysis which was at the core of your legal education. You will see this over time." And I did.

This had been my first extended evening conference with Mr. BB, and those that came thereafter were the most important of my professional life. They were informative, formative, insightful, and profound, and they shaped me and my life as a lawyer and later as a law professor. But even more, they were exhilarating and constituted my most enjoyable moments as a lawyer. Typically, they would begin with a knock on his open door, as I had gotten beyond my childhood stopovers peering silently into his office. As he looked up and saw me, I would begin. "Mr. BB, excuse me, have you had a chance to read my memorandum of law on the Booker lawsuit, and my recommended strategies and arguments on Booker's behalf?"

"Ellie, yes I have, is there anything you wish to discuss?"

"Mr. BB, just wondering. I'm a bit concerned. Before you adopt any portion of it, don't you wish to review my research or at least the statutes and some of the cases I cite and rely upon? There is nothing directly on point, and everything I have done and conclude rests upon analogous fact patterns, issues, and law."

"Ellie, I like what you have done and have been meaning to tell you exactly that. Your work is 'right on,' and I have also been meaning to tell you that."

"But Mr. BB, how do you know that without more? Without, at least, examining my source materials?"

"Ellie, I KNOW! And here is why."

Mr. BB would then begin a dialogue that focused on me and my memorandum, but it also included conversations with himself in which he asked and answered his own important questions. His dialogue, which was essentially a critique, consisted of a meticulous step-by-step dissection of the problem. We would work through an idea, an analogy, a principle, a decision, a statute, a concept, or a strategy again and again until we — I stress we, because he always made it seem like a joint adventure — firmly believed that our analysis and solution were on solid ground and made perfect sense. And, if at first it did not make sense, we retreated further to a conclusion or principle more basic and solid before moving forward towards a goal only then embraced with absolute confidence. Mr. BB stressed good sense, especially when it came to matters of persuasion. Sophistication and erudition were important, but good sense was always paramount. This was his approach to law, business, and to life. And each time we conferred in this manner, I knew the importance of the experience. I knew my good fortune. Mr. BB was not only my best teacher, but maybe the best ever.

These were my most satisfying moments in the practice of law and my time with Mann and Berenz. However, things changed significantly when a third name was added and the law firm became Mann, Berenz, and Kane. Stuart Kane became a partner because of my mother. Unlike either Mann or Berenz, he came from a prominent and privileged background and was a graduate of Harvard College. He was also heavily imbued with Preparation H. Stuart was younger, came to law school and the practice in middle age after a career in business, and was already a rainmaker who could share some of the responsibilities my mother had taken on for herself. Unsaid at least until her son was ready to take over. Kane was full of personality and, often, of himself. Women liked him, maybe even loved him. He was short, overweight, and had a million stories about himself, most untrue. He had opinions on everything, especially the law, including matters without foundation. He loved to talk and expound but not always listen. Stuart Kane enjoyed being at the center of everything important. And he came to the partnership with a book of business, much of which was show business that was not necessarily profitable. At the core of his business were big time novelists, journalists, nightclubs, and entertainers that included actors, actresses, singers (mainly jazz and folk), and comics. These people were exciting. I enjoyed hanging out with them and the many clients who enjoyed their presence especially over drinks at the venue of their performance. Additionally, Kane had non-celebrity clients who came to him for business and corporate matters, estate planning and probate, marriage dissolutions, and litigation issues that touched on many things.

Interacting with celebrities was the exciting part, picking up after Stuart Kane was not. In short, he was not a craftsman. Stuart felt more like a disaster waiting to happen. He was not the lawyer I had known in my mother and Mr. BB, and certainly not the lawyer I wanted to become. He was a master of flying by the seat of his pants and shooting from the hip. He enjoyed spouting information and announcing clear-cut solutions, all without experience or knowledge that would support the confidence that underlied his many pronouncements. His files were incomplete, and his research was often nonexistent. All of that would be laid on my lap, and it was my job to give substance, execution, and completion to tasks and positions he had staked out as doable. You could seldom pin him down on the why or basis for anything. Stuart Kane marched through life and lawyering as if the problems one leaves behind either go unnoticed or simply disappear over time. Somehow all things heal over or eventually disappear. Yet I had been taught the opposite in law school and by both Mann and Berenz of Mann and Berenz. Lawyers were problem solvers at essence, and their mission was to identify problems, define them, and resolve them. And certainly not to ignore them! Their legal prescriptions never involved the equivalent of "take two aspirin and get some rest." Direct action, sometimes discreet and understated, was almost always required. Inevitably, my frustration, stress, and unhappiness mounted over several months.

But I wasn't the only one. Mann and Berenz had three secretaries, one for Mann, one for Berenz, and a swing secretary who took me on after I arrived. Later, Stuart was added to her responsibilities with overflow to be assumed by the other two. Stuart made life hell for her, because she too had to pick up the pieces and launder his dirty work. His written notes for letters, documents, and everything else were indecipherable. And when he wasn't using written notes, he was dictating with sentences that had to be rewritten and paragraphs that were nonexistent. Our secretary was first rate and also outspoken. Occasionally she would simply throw her hands up in the air in his presence as if to say "what now." Stuart was offended: "Stop terrorizing and abusing me. I am the lawyer and you are not!" It was time for another session with Mr. BB.

"Mr. BB, what am I supposed to do with the work Stuart dumps on my lap? His files are a mess, and his directions are often confused, misguided, and impossible to implement, often because of the law, practicality, or reality. He piles it on day after day. He gives advice, pronounces strategies, files lawsuits, and I must cope with the consequences. Help!"

Mr. BB looked up from his desk, shrugged his shoulders, and took a deep breath before rising from his chair and closing his office door (which, beginning with my childhood recollections, was always wide open). Then he asked me to sit down and pulled up a chair beside me. For the first time I saw Mr. BB as older, even aging; more grey hair and more facial wrinkles and lines. For the first time, I witnessed fatigue reflected in his face and body language. And before speaking, there was a long pause as if to wonder what he should share and say. "Ellie, it's not good. You are not the only one disturbed and stressed, nor are you the only one picking up after him. Some of his clients recognize and acknowledge this, so now they call your mother or me directly even late at night. We both agree this has been a failed experiment to expand our business and relieve some of the rainmaking pressure on your mother. Right now we have no immediate plan, yet this cannot continue. We both know it for certain. I am confident we will part ways with Stuart soon enough, but for now you must be patient, however much that hurts. Meanwhile, look at the bright side; you now know much about how not to practice law." Until then his expression and demeanor had been grim; finally, the familiar and comforting smile.

"But Mr. BB, why hasn't my mother shared and discussed this with me? She has declared, again and again, that my destiny is with Mann and Berenz, which has now become my present and future. If there is a crisis, I should know about it from the inside, not merely the outside. Inevitably, there is no way to shield me from the crisis or its consequences."

Mr BB's reply was unusually direct—even scolding—but also insightful. "Ellie, don't make this about you. It's no time to whine. She is your mother and also your employer. As to an employer, I know of no one who would have done differently. And as for a mother, these kinds of conversations are often difficult and painful. Part of her may wish to shield you from this dilemma; part of her may not want to admit poor judgment. You are an adult, young and destined for success, but you are still her 'boy.' She is still responsible for you. You are independent but still dependent on her, and that's the way she views it and wants it. This may continue indefinitely, no matter how established and successful you become. And if you both live long enough, there will be a time for reckoning and role reversal. She will become your dependent and lean heavily upon your love and care. Ellie, one more thing. I have no difficulty speaking with you and sharing most anything. I almost think of you as a peer and not that four year old boy I first knew. In many respects, the openness and bonding this requires is easier between a young person and people other than parents. Trust me, one day you may find it easier to communicate with the counterparts in age of your children and eventually even your grandchildren—and more important, so might they with you—than your own children and grandchildren. Quite simply, there isn't the same baggage inevitable to child-rearing and the emotional investment it demands. Thankfully, I didn't have to deal with your toddler tantrums or teenage rants, and you avoided my parental rigidity, rules, protestations, and repeated groundings. Just think of the quite different relationship you and I have and also the relationship between students and teachers in all kinds of contexts. Preschool, primary grades, high school, college, graduate school, coaches and players, you name it. In each instance, the worries are less for the teacher or coach, the time is less, and the investment is less, but often the candor, openness and sharing is greater. Ellie, this is life. Get over it." This was another of Mr. BBs important life lessons, something I would better understand, appreciate, and utilize over the next fifty years.

2 | THE BEST TEACHER I HAVE EVER KNOWN

My next passage in life was a total surprise, both as to opportunity and timing. But it was also a surprise as to abilities and confidence, because I felt I had neither and was not ready for this opportunity. I received a letter from the Eliot University School of Law inviting me to apply for a position on their faculty. The School anticipated enrollment increases to accommodate post-War baby boomers soon to enter law school, and they wanted to stay ahead of the curve in hiring the best young faculty available. So they contacted my law school and several others and asked for names of several graduates from recent years whom they would highly recommend for teaching. And my name was among them. I read it in disbelief. ME? No way. The law professors I admired most were larger than life; brilliant, nimble, articulate, clever, humorous, and could command the subject and orchestrate class discussion with perfect tempo and harmony. This required, at the very least, time, experience, and expertise. And I was short on every count. In what subject was I an expert? None. After several days, I deposited the letter in my waste basket at home. By then, Berke and I had married and were soon to have a child. She found the letter and confronted me. I explained. If I would ever be prepared to teach, it wasn't now, it was somewhere in the future. I knew I enjoyed research and writing and could really do it, but the classroom was another matter. Berke listened carefully and said: "WHY NOT!"

"BECAUSE, because I am not ready! I am a master of nothing and have no teaching experience or even public speaking or debate in my past or present. And that's it!"

"Randy, I have faith. I know you can do it, and the time for adventure and chance in our lives is now. So let's begin this journey with a new life and new lives ahead. Please! Go share this news immediately with your mother."

Which I did, still unsure of whether I was capable of making this leap. My mother's reaction was different than what I expected, yet no surprise. "Ellie this is great news. What an honor. A Professor! Go ahead, do it. Apply for the position and get the job. In a few years, you can return with prestige and cache for Mann and Berenz that one can't buy. Our own in-house Professor, our built-in expert. I know you will want to return to your destiny and that you will."

Mr. BB's reaction was different. Looking back, it should have been expected, but it wasn't. "Ellie, this is great news. What an honor! A Professor. Go ahead, do it! Apply for the position and get the job. Ellie, you have found your destiny; it is the life you were meant for and must pursue full throttle. Go for it. I know you well, you will succeed!"

So I applied, got the job, packed up six months later, and left with Berke and an infant daughter for Eliot University. I was given a standard four course load in subjects in which I had had no experience or long-standing interest. This was also standard for the times. But it did include a first year course, which is what I had wanted most. My first year of teaching was overwhelming but exciting. A minimum of ten hours of preparation for every hour of class and never more than two weeks ahead of the syllabus. I learned a subject and how to conduct classes on the fly. I could even see myself becoming the teacher I wanted to become. And there was something immediate that I never antic-ipated: palpable and positive chemistry with students within and beyond the classroom. Connections that enriched their learning and mine, connections that ultimately yielded life-long friendships. Thirty days into my first semester, I knew I wasn't returning to Mann and Berenz or the practice of law. I KNEW my destiny. Once again, Mr. BB was right. Once again, Mr. BB understood me better than I did.

Even though I never hid my joy and commitment to teaching, my mother was disappointed when I did not return to Mann and Berenz after two years of teaching. Eventually, she accepted my decision. Eventually, she was very pleased with my success. But she never took my name off the door to Mann and Berenz, at least not until they merged with a large firm (one of the many that would never have hired her out of law school) several years later. The merger was without Stuart Kane and a huge relief. It was also the first stage of eventual retirement without a son to carry on the business, without a son des-tined to annuitize her future. In later years, my mother loved reading everything I authored, coming to class, watching me teach, raising her hand, and contributing to the discussion. At first, I did my utmost to keep her quiet; then I simply gave up and enjoyed every moment as I fully recognized and ap-preciated her brilliance and insight. And so did the students.

When we returned home to visit my mother and father, I would always call Mr. BB and sometimes see him over lunch. Still a tuna sandwich and coffee, still a burger, turkey instead of beef, nothing on it, but no chocolate milkshake. Just a glass full without the metal container was never the same and no longer my beverage of choice. Mr. BB was in basic retirement but still active. He had moved to another large firm that gave him an office and support. This enabled him to continue work on behalf of a handful of his long-time clients and to mentor young lawyers at the firm. Eventually in full retirement, he moved to another firm simply to become a mentor in residence. These visits were always warm and encouraging. His interest in everything and the power of his intellect had not changed. And he always governed our conversations as he had throughout.

These recurrent visits ceased after Mr. BB reached his late eighties and moved to the Twin Cities to be near his adult children. However, our correspondence and reviews of everything I wrote continued. He was, as always, perceptive, insightful, intelligent, eloquent, and kind. This continued until one day, Berke said to me: "Isn't it time for another session with Mr. BB? I have never been to Minnesota in the summer, and I would like to visit. So let's do it, Randy, before it's too late."

So we contacted him, drove to the Twin Cities, and arranged a reunion over lunch with Mr. BB and his wife. At age ninety-two, he was no longer driving. We picked them up and proceeded to a favorite restaurant of theirs. The lunch was lengthy—much like our evening sessions at Mann and Berenz—and rewarding. As usual, I learned much, especially about making the most of life no matter the age. Mr. BB lived on the twelfth floor of a twenty-two story building. He almost always avoided the elevator when leaving or returning to his condominium. He preferred stairs above all, and once a week, he walked all twenty-two floors. He read from plays of Shakespeare daily, and worked at memorizing sonnets. He also read and studied every opinion of the U.S. Supreme Court (and sometimes the briefs of the parties involved), and finally he would compose—in long-hand of course—his own concurring or dissenting opinion. Mr. BB did this until age ninety-five when he died suddenly of an aneurism. And I wept for the best teacher I have ever known.

———————

Not long before Mr. BB died, he sent me his review of my recent book on Theories, Strategies, and Methodologies for Legal Analysis, Issues, and Argumentation. It was, as always, in long-hand, pen and ink. After some minor criticisms, he said that many of the top legal scholars of the twentieth century would have been proud to have authored this book. Although I wanted and sought his praise, it was over the top. Yet I knew he meant it even though I had not earned it. And then he offered this addendum to the importance of analytic skills and the essence of legal education.

"One may think of the body of all the law as an immense granary. In law school, grain—law knowledge or information—is delivered to the students. But the grain must be ground, else unusable, and a mill is needed to do the grinding. Analytic skill is the mill. Analytic skill does the grinding that makes the grain usable. Much/most of the knowledge gained in law school is forgotten.... But analytic skill is a mode, a way of *thinking*. That skill becomes sharper with use, and once impressed upon a brain—unlike knowledge/learned facts—should stay within that brain for life. So the law school must do more than deliver grain. It must deliver the mill which grinds the grain and makes it usable.... Not only does analytical skill once acquired stay with one for life, but that skill is infinitely flexible, and so can 'grind,' so to speak, an infinite variety of grains, or putting the matter more plainly, analytic skill enables the lawyer/student to deal with an infinite variety of law problems. Law knowledge without analytic skill is an unusable product."

We all depend upon others for who we are and who we become. We stand upon and rise up from their shoulders to achievements unexpected, even unimagined. Parents, grandparents, friends, teachers. I stand upon the shoulders of many, but without Mr. BB, I would never have slammed dunk a basketball or even touched the rim.

CHAPTER 3

MY FAVORITE COLLEAGUE

E. Randall Mann

In over fifty years of teaching at the Eliot School of Law, I have had many colleagues, not too numerous to count, yet too difficult to easily reconstruct. This much I do recall. I began with a faculty of nine at the Eliot School of Law and years later we reached our high water mark of seventy, though we are fewer today. Faculty members come and go, and one must get used to this, especially the loss of best friends. Comparatively few remain for the long haul, especially for a career, perhaps more at Eliot than elsewhere. Eliot City is a great place to live and raise a family. Easy walking distance (or even driving distance) to most anything, including my workplace and my children's schools of many years ago. As for me, I have been a lifer, Eliot has been my lifetime professional home, and without regret. And as I look around, a few others may ripen into lifers as well. Fifty years is a long time, actually it's fifty-one. Yes, I have seen many go. A lot to retirement and ultimately death. A fair number to failed attempts at tenure, either actual or inevitable. And many to other schools and to greener pastures, or so it seemed. I suppose this turnover is true of other businesses, though in academia, it's primarily the tenured employee's choice and not the employer. Some departures do not feel like much has been lost, instead sometimes a gain. While others seem like a huge setback from which the school may never recover. As to the latter, I'll not forget the sobering comments of a wise colleague: "Randy, no one ever eclipses the institution; it is forever. Teachers and administrators come and go and over time are forgotten. Although the course of an institution may be influenced by specific people, it is dependent upon the presence of no one."

Any story about colleagues is a remembrance of important people, at least to me. Most departures, inevitable or not, felt like a huge and unsurmountable loss. Some of the other departures were a relief; bigots, sexual opportunists, racists, and arrogant prima donnas who thought of nothing but themselves and their careers and would step on anyone in their path. And they would attempt to justify with sweet reason everything that was self-serving. No surprise, lawyers and especially law professors are gifted at rationalizing most everything. Nevertheless, my grandmother once advised, as she did on many things: "Ellie, if you have nothing good to say about someone, then don't say it." I suffered when my parents named me Ellsworth, that's what the initial E is for, and I didn't like being called Ellie quite apart from Ellsworth, which was worse. Certainly not by them. But my grandmother was different, always both kind and wise, or so it seemed. I never could bring myself to refuse her "Ellie" or her advice. If I were to reject her advice and instead include tales of sexual affairs with students, incompetence, and hate, this story might sell better. But the message in each would be much too obvious; stories of "no-no's" that most have heard before. Yet I am a teacher who likes to teach and also to recount, especially with things positive derived from personal experience. And so I would like to say something good about a particular colleague; something about a person who has given me much and from whom I have learned much. Something about my dear friend and favorite colleague.

ROGER DAVIS

Looking back I don't remember the first time I met Roger Davis. After receiving my job offer from the Eliot School of Law, I was invited to the campus to meet the entire faculty, the Chancellor of the University and others. Roger said it was then. I simply don't remember. But I do recall our getting to know each other after I had accepted the offer and moved to Eliot City the following summer. Typically, five or six of the faculty of nine, including me, would lunch together at least three days a week. The composition might change, but not its leader—Roger Davis. Roger selected the restaurants and the time of departure. I saw it as a faculty ritual and almost always tagged along hoping to learn something. And I did. The best part occurred after we had returned to the law school and Roger would get his cup of coffee and I would follow, even though I did not like coffee, at least not then.

Roger was not much older than I, although he always seemed older than not much. He made the cut for WWII, which I just missed. That gave him instant credibility, especially for a teen that had followed and studied every island invasion in the South Pacific in newspaper and movie tone news accounts. Roger had the unmistakable aura of a leader. He stood well over six feet and appeared even taller with the posture of a U.S. Marine, which he had been, always at attention. He was not only tall but muscled as well, and in unbelievable condition. He had been an outstanding athlete, but at age forty, his attention turned to fitness instead of competition. Each morning, he did the Royal Canadian Exercises designed for members of the Canadian Air Force. Roger conquered each level of fitness in record time and was maintaining their most demanding routine at 5:00 A.M. daily. He loved sports and fitness and to talk about both. But above all, his talk focused on teaching, because Roger was an accomplished teacher of both students and teachers. And so our after lunch coffee sessions were my introduction to what it meant to be a real teacher. I had my models always in mind, best teachers from law school and the best teacher I have known, Mr. BB from childhood. But Roger gave me direction in how to get to where I wanted to go: a Socratic teacher who could lead and orchestrate an entire class much like the best of symphony conductors, yet pedagogical goals would always be achieved by the hard work of the players, namely those tasked to learn.

As I recall, it all began with a simple question: "Randy, have you adopted a casebook for your course on Property?"

"That's exactly what I am struggling with, Roger. And I can't seem to make up my mind. I have received copies of all the books from all of the publishers, and I have examined each, but still can't decide. I know I have to decide within the week. So at the moment, I am leaning toward the book my teacher of property used. Although my teacher was not a favorite, familiarity makes it a comfortable choice."

"Randy, not necessarily. Do you see any difference among the books?"

"Roger, I only observed two differences, book length and number of cases despite the same course. And shorter looked better to me because I could get through it."

"Randy, that's not reason enough. This past December, I attended a panel discussion at the annual meeting of the Association of American Law Schools. The discussion focused on two new casebooks in criminal law. One was three hundred pages and the other seven hundred. The two presenters were the two authors. After many questions from other members of the panel and the audience, the author of the shorter book asked the other: 'Do you really discuss all six hundred pages of materials in one semester?' And the other answered: 'Absolutely. There are coverage cases and cases for more extended critical analysis. That's how. But I am teaching analytic skills throughout.' The reply to that was: 'Impossible, you can't teach critical thinking and analysis for all six hundred pages of cases in that time frame. I'll bet you're lecturing most of the time.' The two did not come to blows, but that was the last conversation between them. Randy, simply stated: your book choice must reflect what you wish to accomplish in the course." And with that, Roger changed the subject and began asking how Berke, my wife, and Laura, our infant daughter, were adjusting to life in Eliot City.

Two days later, after lunch and on the way to coffee, Roger continued his inquiry. Roger was known as a master teacher and carried the nickname of "The Bear." But never a teddy bear, more nearly a Grizzly. Although his questions reflected Socratic skills, he never was overbearing with me enough to resemble "The Bear." Just a friend urging me to reflect on the why of what I was attempting to do. But this time I began with a question. "Roger, I have been asking around with other colleagues about books and what coverage I should achieve daily. After all, once I make my book selection, I have to prepare a syllabus reflecting daily assignments. Ralph Livingston said three cases a day at a minimum. Richard Warren said one section of a chapter daily, usually more than three cases. And Willy Greenfield told me to simply divide the number of book pages by the number of classes to be taught and the answer to that should govern. Roger what do you think? Should I adopt Ralph's method?"

"Randy, it depends."

"Richard's?"

"It depends."

"Willy's?"

"It depends!"

"On what?"

"Randy, on what you wish to accomplish in the course."

"Roger, is your answer to all of my big concerns the same?"

"Randy, it's inevitably the place to begin the search for one's self as a teacher."
That was little consolation.

"So, Roger, what does your syllabus look like?"

"I don't have one."

"You don't have one!"

"Yes, I always know where I want to begin and have a vague idea of where I want to conclude, but I don't feel compelled to arrive there. I let the substance and discussion of each class dictate progress. If something unexpected arises that's worth pursuing—often an idea or commentary that's fresh and exciting—I simply pursue it and exhaust it even if it takes the entire class hour or the next and sometimes the next. Because I have been doing this for many years and because I want the classroom discussion and dynamic to trump all else, I usually end up at the same place with the same coverage. Yet there are years in which novel discussions and analyses dominate and coverage contracts, and my solution is always the same. Draft an exam that fits materials actually covered. Consequently, I don't focus on ambition; instead, it's on reality and, most of all, successful pursuit of pedagogical objectives." Roger's comments resonated, but left me uncomfortable. I wanted to be a Socratic teacher who taught the transcendent skills of problems solving, and I had experienced teachers who modeled how to achieve them. But I was uncertain and uneasy with the nuts and bolts of the craft. I needed things concrete, like a syllabus. Did I ever have a course in college or law school without something resembling a syllabus? A syllabus (or even a brief outline) inevitably focused on reading assignments, even those without timelines. Isn't this a teacher's effort to achieve coverage? Yet for me, it was also a security blanket. So I adopted the book with the fewest number of cases and pages. Three cases a day, as Ralph had commanded, would get me through the entire casebook, and I was confident I could do it. And I prepared an elaborate syllabus expressed in terms of weekly assignments for the four class hours conducted each week. And then I prepared the first three weeks of assignments and nervously awaited my first class. The syllabus gave me some comfort, and the three weeks of preparation assured me I could stay ahead of the class if I didn't outpace my three cases a day approach. If I went too fast, another concern! What if I covered everything with two weeks to go in the semester? More to worry about, and I did.

The first several weeks went well. Coverage with three cases a day worked perfectly even though class discussion was perfunctory and uninspiring both for me and the students. But then my life as a teacher changed with a student's questions, ones that I did not anticipate. It was a question during office hours asked by "Mr. Stamp," who had knocked on the door, entered, and plopped himself down in my easy chair used primarily for power naps. His expressions and demeanor were no-nonsense, business-like, and very serious. And he did not budge, because class discussion and his extensive thought, research, and analysis devoted to course materials had inspired many questions. He had gone beyond formal reading assignments and reached tentative conclusions to these questions on his own, and he wanted my time to explore and challenge his analyses. For only a moment I felt put-upon and resistant, but then I realized that his response to class discussion was exactly what I had hoped to inspire: a capacity to self-educate and problem solve. So two consecutive afternoons were devoted to Mr. Stamp's questions, hypotheses and resolutions as we addressed issues neither of us had considered before.

Immediately afterward, I knocked on Roger's door, and explained what had happened. "Randy, that's exciting and truly an exhilarating moment for a teacher. Don't you wish it had emerged, at least in part, in class?"

"Yes, and for more than one reason. Our discussion was exactly the kind of experience I had hoped to create in class, a kind of group exploration orchestrated by teacher questions and guidance. Further, the quality of our discussion was so illustrative of what legal education is about that I wanted the entire class to share the experience."

"Randy, then make it so, just use your imagination as to how you can prime the pump so that these things arise naturally or you can force-feed them when they do not. Meanwhile, you must realize the consequence of these extended classroom explorations. They will destroy your quest for three cases daily and any time table attached to a syllabus. Extended time for critical thinking and analytic skills—time commitments that arise for spontaneous detours, especially those one might wish to incorporate permanently—inevitably take a toll on coverage. If critical thinking and transcendent analytical skills are at the core of what you wish to achieve, then allow them to shape the courses you teach. And if you do, be prepared for less and less coverage—always less than the book and even your syllabus—at least for several times through the same course. And don't give it another thought." And that's what I did, although I did give it another thought and usually felt guilty for not accomplishing everything.

Before my first semester ended, and not long before exams, I asked Roger if I could visit his class, and without hesitation, he said YES. Roger selected any of three days during the following week and gave me copies of the cases and statutes probably discussed. And then with a smile, he assured me that he would not call on me. I asked him whether I might attend all three, and again his answer was YES. And so I appeared at all three. The first class began with Roger immediately calling upon a student: "Mr. Blackwell, please tell us about the Smithson Case." It was the first case of a new chapter. Roger gave no introductory preface, summary, or context, nor was there any attempt to connect what came before with the new chapter or with anything that came thereafter. Just a cold turkey beginning. And then silence. Roger simply repeated: "Mr. Blackwell, would you PLEASE tell us about the Smithson Case." I was seated behind Mr. Blackwell and could not witness his expression. Yet I didn't have too. More silence. I simply knew. Roger folded his arms and stood still. More silence that seemed forever for Mr. Blackwell and eventually for all. Roger then asked: "Mr. Blackwell, have your read the Smithson Case?" More silence as Mr. Blackwell looked down at his feet.

Finally, he said: "I am sorry sir, I have not. Yesterday was a busy day for me."

Roger replied: "I am certain it was for everyone here, yesterday and every day in law school. As it should be. Well the case is merely two pages, so we will wait while you read it now. If this seems harsh, it is a lot less than what I observed in school when teachers banished those who were unprepared from the classroom or walked out themselves and abandoned the class." Immediately there were gasps throughout the classroom followed by absolute silence. The only sound heard over the next ten minutes was from Mr. Blackwell turning page one to page two of the Smithson Case. Finally, Mr. Blackwell looked up at Roger who nodded in acknowledgment that they were both ready to proceed. "Mr. Blackwell, now then, how about the facts of the Smithson Case?"

Mr. Blackwell began slowly reciting facts and then he paused. Roger then asked a question that redirected Mr. Blackwell's focus and recitation of additional facts. Thereafter, Mr. Blackwell paused again. Roger then asked: "Mr. Blackwell, I think you have exhausted relevant facts, now tell me what is the issue or issues in this case?" Mr. Blackwell stumbled, but continued with the issues, relevant law and its application, and additional hypotheticals presented by Roger that tested the wisdom of controlling principles and underlying policy. Mr. Blackwell responded to everything as Roger attempted to guide him and the class up the mountain of critical thinking and analysis. Every time Mr. Blackwell stumbled, Roger backed him down the mountain to a plateau with secure footing and understanding that Mr. Blackwell could command. And then Roger would once again march him up the mountain. Up the mountain, then sometimes back, and finally all the way until the mountain peak had been scaled. This took the entire class hour. Students left in silence.

I was also silent as I returned to my office, mainly because I was stunned. I knew that I wanted to be like Roger, but not entirely. I wanted to be the teacher who brilliantly led Mr. Blackwell up the mountain, but not the one who waited endlessly, or so it seemed, for him to speak before their journey began. Roger had delivered a message, but it was not mine. Was Mr. Blackwell really unprepared? Somehow I felt that his silence was rooted in terror, and avoidance was his best pathway to relief. In the end, Mr. Blackwell might have been grateful for Roger's persistence and heavy hand. After all, Mr. Blackwell did reach the summit by mounting an analysis and performance that achieved success. He may have known it and, more importantly, felt it. But others may not have experienced and acknowledged it. And with that, there may have been a cost in which some students were lost to overwhelming terror. This was something I didn't want to risk. Besides, it just wasn't me. I did not discuss my reactions to his class with Roger for several years. I was struggling to find myself as a teacher and wanted to sort things out first. And I did so mainly by groping my way. One thing became immediately clear. I was not a coverage person. Three cases a day failed me, and each course syllabus was amended to cover something less. Over time, I came to realize who I was as a teacher, someone related to Roger but not conceived by him.

Roger and I continued to talk about teaching, but with less frequency. We did, however, discuss my first set of exams, especially their formulation and grading. Roger preferred a series of short essays with limited and carefully targeted issues. They were easier to assess and, therefore, to grade. They reminded me of bar exam questions in which I was tempted to find more to discuss than was ever intended. So I began to experiment with just three questions for an exam lasting three hours. Each had a story much like the one a client might tell, a story with things relevant and irrelevant. And each story was concocted by working backwards from the legal principles and issues I wished to test and interconnect. And at least one of the three would take the students beyond what they knew and test their ability to apply their skill-set beyond their comfort zone. Roger read my first draft of my first exam carefully and with interest. "Randy, it's brilliant, but it's trouble. It's going to be a nightmare to grade." And it was. And still is as I attempt to make each final exam a new learning experience, something more than required teacher assessment; foolishly, perhaps. I hold out hope each term for an exam that illustrates and punctuates the semester's worth of learning experience. Grading never gets easier. Berke, my wife, always said that my personality changed to something well beyond grumpy and the importance of the task. It never threatened my marriage, perhaps almost.

During the spring semester of that first year of teaching, Roger's soft Socratic inquiry turned to research and writing. "Randy, what are your plans this summer?"

"Roger, I'm beginning to really know you, and I KNOW you don't mean family vacation."

"Randy, I don't wish to exclude important things like family vacations."

"Roger, but getting to the heart of your question, I have an idea that I wish to pursue that concerns the rule against perpetuities."

"The Rule! When I had to teach a Future Interests Course, that was my downfall. In my day, most every young teacher had to teach courses throughout the curriculum, and I was determined to never teach it again. But why Randy are you making that your first effort at scholarship? Something arcane and something almost no one understands?"

"Roger, precisely because of the latter; no one understands it, not really. Not even practicing lawyers, judges, and even law teachers, at least the ones that taught me. More accurately, I should say no one can explain it adequately, not even those who can apply it. Many can achieve correct conclusions and even explain to others the basis for their proof of validity or invalidity. These explanations work by way of solutions to specific problems. They provide insight, yet they work backward. They do not look forward. They do not empower students or lawyers to solve problems not already solved or explained. No one has really formalized a process for solving something previously unseen, at least something unseen by the problem solver. This is a challenge that fascinates me."

Roger took a deep breath, thought for a moment of what he wanted to say, and how to say it. And then he began with a message of no nonsense. "Randy, don't do it. You can't make it your first piece of scholarship. Paradigm changers come later. You may be up to this, but almost no one is, at least with the time table attached to tenure requirements for publications. I warn you. Don't attempt this, not now. This kind of piece requires maturity as a teacher and scholar. Just think of what you might learn from your students. At the very least, whatever process you conceive can be tested in the classes you teach. Randy, it's your personal laboratory. Ideas need to evolve and percolate, and you cannot depend upon overnight success. You clearly don't want to be treading water with nothing to show for it when your first tenure evaluations occur." The tone of Roger's message and voice had changed to something I had not seen. Soft Socratic morphed into loud declaratives. Roger then paused as if he had heard himself and observed a mentor much too directive. He had voiced disapproval with something I really wanted to do.

"Roger, learn from students? Aren't things the other way around? Surely, I can't delay this kind of enterprise with the hope of eliciting insight from students regarding a formula no one has discovered."

"Randy, yes you can. Someday you will realize that many of your best ideas come from students, triggered by questions, comments, and glimpses of ideas not yet considered. Randy, yes you can and must." This was his most important message, what students give to teachers, my discovery and personal mantra of years later. However, I did not listen then. But I did two years later.

I had a stubborn streak in me, seldom seen by others yet still there. I always felt this stubbornness was a towering asset, not a weakness. I thought of it as persistence, the grit that got me through tough times in school and in ballgames. I could out work and out play others because of unrelenting determination and focus. Giving up was never an option. I might attribute this to something genetic, but parental commandments were a more obvious source. (Maybe they are one and the same.) "Never be a quitter" was my mother's mantra, and in later years, my father's as well. Though he had given up as an architect in the early 1930s when builders ceased building, and never returned to it post World War II, he still bought into the mantra, and still screamed at his son—the pitcher, with bases loaded and no outs—"don't ever quit on your team." I still hear those words, a memory and a beacon that live brightly. This family mantra seldom got me in trouble, but it did when I paid no heed to Roger Davis's advice.

Tenure is a tricky thing. Faculty tenure documents offer broad descriptions about matters of teaching, scholarship, and service. The first two are critical, while the third is sometimes ignored. Although at elite schools, some might say: So is the first, at least when the scholarship is spectacular. Regardless, scholarship means everything. No surprise then that entry level teachers always have the same important questions, often phrased differently, yet always the same. How many publications, what expectations as to quality (must all be paradigm shifting), and how long? The answers have recurrent themes, yet the emphasis might vary, and no two faculty members ever wish to say the same thing, at least never in the same way. I listened to all of this, but I did not hear. At least not clearly enough to shift direction. After my second year at Eliot, it was time for review of my progress towards promotion with tenure. But after hour after hour of research and thought and reams and reams of notes, I had nothing to show for it except theories that failed to explain the Rule. No acceptance for publication of a manuscript from a prestigious law review or for that matter from any law review. I did not even have a first draft. Nothing! This was deemed unacceptable by the faculty tenure committee. Despite excellent teaching evaluations, I was warned. The tenure track that leads up to tenure is always called the probationary period. And I was really deemed on probation with a time clock that seemed destined to expire.

I was scared, really scared. When I left the practice to begin a career in teaching, my fears focused on the classroom and not the production of scholarship. I was scared, really scared, with the thought of conducting a class with the skill of a symphonic conductor who leads but leaves the making of music to orchestral players, something I had witnessed in the best of my law school teachers who had mastered the Socratic Method. At the outset, this fear was disabling when I ended my first class fifteen minutes after it had begun while faking my way out the room with a lame excuse. But because Berke commanded, even rehearsed, immediate return to the saddle, I was in class the next day and, best of all, finished it and soon came to enjoy it. The fear was understandable. I had had no relevant experience, and like most law teachers, the first class was the first time. But writing papers, articles, and even books never inspired fear, nor was the task daunting. I was good at it, and there was a reason. Experience and lots of it. I gravitated to college and law school courses with papers, even to some with book length requirements like an honors thesis. Most important, I never had difficulty finding a thesis or developing something original. And by the time I began teaching, I was confident that these ideas would always surface. This was my reason for teaching, and it was something I knew I could do.

And then this review by the tenure committee. I was off track and destined for failure after pursuing something much-too-much against good advice. The ideas may have been percolating and soon emergent, yet the project was impractical. Time requirements exist for everything, especially tenure tracks. Or more fundamentally, maybe I was plain wrong. My problem was more than miscalculation. Was I now in a league beyond reach? A league in which the ideas I might spin out were unworkable or worse. Simplistic. Unoriginal. Un-

sophisticated. Unworthy. And undeserving of a university's lifetime commitment. I retreated to my office after being told and then reminded I was on probation, sat down, and sulked for two hours. I called Berke and asked her to go
ahead with dinner because of an unexpected meeting. And I sulked, all the
while feeling sorry for myself. Purposely I did not return home until after Berke
was asleep. I already knew what she would say. Berke was strong-minded. She
was a doer who could focus on a problem, find a solution, and forge ahead.
All problems had solutions, provided one had will power. And will power was
something she always assumed for everyone, because for Berke, it underscored
her very being. I could hear her voice: "Randy, you have the ability, you always
have, now just do it. From me you need encouragement, better yet a kick in
the pants." Not doing something one wanted to do was inexcusable especially
if it was doable because one had the ability to do exactly that. Not doing was
sinful and evidence of a lack of character. And in Berke's eyes, also grounds
for divorce. So I had no choice. I wanted to succeed in teaching, especially now
that I knew I could conquer the classroom. I arose early the next morning and
left for work as Berke and the children were getting ready for school.

Reluctantly, I then returned to Roger for advice, actually for something
more like a recipe to save the day. After our previous discussion a year earlier
in which he forewarned me, Roger did not discuss the subject of scholarship
with me. I did join him at the faculty lunches he led more often than not, and
we did occasionally have coffee afterward, mostly just the two of us. But I
always deflected meaningful discussion of teaching, research, and writing.
Roger was on the faculty tenure committee that admonished me and warned
me that I was not on track for promotion with tenure, and so he was not surprised to see me at the door to his office. Before I knocked I was prepared to
humble myself and eat crow. But there was no need. Roger did not begin with
any message that sounded like "I told you so." Or "this is your own doing, and
now you ask for help!" Instead, it was "let's get to work." "Randy, what do you
have by way of written work products that I can examine. Anything you have
will help, especially ideas, comments, hypotheses, background. And I mean
anything however rough its shape. Anything that might afford me a glimpse
of what you have examined, discovered, contemplated, or even pushed aside
for a subsequent agenda. Simple as that, now get out of here and get at it." And
I did.

One week later I presented him with everything understandable. I also organized the materials and added some introductions and explanations that in-

troduced a body of problems, research, ideas, and conclusions and also some memoranda that connected work products otherwise seemingly disconnected. I hand delivered them to Roger and then waited for his silver bullet that would rescue me from misguided stubbornness and inevitable failure. The wait was less than a week. This time he knocked on my door. "Randy, I think I have something for you that's immediately doable. A busy summer lies ahead. It means delaying your process for understanding and applying the Rule, but still writing something that focuses on the Rule. Actually, more than one written piece; you can catch up and finish two good ones and, I think, get them done this summer before classes resume." Roger then referred back to my work products and explained how I had already done major work on two fundamental questions concerning the Rule and underlying policy that were natural precursors to my quest for a formula for its easy understanding and application. I had some further questions to which he had both answers and questions. Roger then left. I went to work and essentially didn't see him until the fall when he returned from a visiting summer appointment at another law school. And upon his return, I presented Roger with manuscripts for two law review articles.

Ten days later Roger came by my office late afternoon with my two manuscripts and two memoranda that seemed nearly as long as what I had written. "Randy, this won't take long for me to explain. Your articles are publishable and very good. Well done! You have recovered from a situation that seemed hopeless to many and to some who said it couldn't be done. I am giving you written comments on both pieces. Unlike our earlier discussion, this is simply my advice on how to improve your manuscripts. It is not an admonition and certainly not a command. Please treat it that way. If you have any questions, you know how to reach me." And then he left.

I was overjoyed and called Berke to share the good news. "Randy, you always delay the bad news, like the tenure committee's last decision. Thank goodness for your timely sharing of something happy. It's much better than an early warning that you're returning to law practice. The kids are crying and hungry, so when are you coming home?"

"Berke, not for several hours. I've got to get at Roger's memos immediately."

Both of Roger's memos were long and reflected lots of work and reflection. In it he laid out everything that he thought could be improved. It was exhaustive. I had never seen anything like it before. It included comments that were conceptual in nature. Along with those that focused on organization. Those that tested logic, clarity, and conclusions, along with those that questioned syntax, punctuation, and grammar. Anything and everything was there for me to consider. Just that was impressive enough. Yet what struck me the most was his approach. Roger never said anything that resembled: "Here is the way I would write an article on this subject. Now do as I would do." He didn't say it and didn't imply it. Instead, he read my manuscripts carefully, determined what I was trying to do, and how I was going to do it. And then Roger concluded that it worked. Finally, even though he might have written his own article on the subject differently and, perhaps, better, he directed me in great detail as to how I could make what I wanted to accomplish even better. And so it was that, prior to publication, I became committed: that everything I wrote thereafter was to go through Roger's editorial hands. And it did until the day he died. Roger had been my mentor. Good mentors are exceptional teachers. That much I already knew and had experienced with Roger during my initial year of teaching. But these memos brought into focus Roger's greatest strengths and a premise that I had to embrace and pursue. Teachers as mentors of teachers or teachers of students can seldom transform, at least not completely. Their subjects simply are who they are, shaped by experience, education, even genetics. Mentee-teachers and students in law school are adults and essentially fully formed. Seldom can a mentor rewrite or recast his subject. Success is best accomplished within a context, the context of strengths, weaknesses, and personality. Something to be partnered not ignored. Roger had understood this and had mastered all of it. And his first step in the process, always his first step, was to listen intently. Nothing could be accomplished without it.

My tenure promotion from assistant professor to associate professor occurred less than a year later. In completing my two manuscripts and preparing them for publication, Roger read and commented on every draft. And he seemed to thoroughly enjoy celebrating both my publications and promotion. But after that, an unexpected distance emerged. His mentoring, both subtle and overt, from the day I arrived at Eliot created a kind of closeness. It felt like a great friendship. He was for me like an older brother, something I had never had. We continued to see each other frequently, but only at the faculty lunch excursions he led several times a week and at dinner parties at faculty homes. Our conversations were always cordial and friendly. But it wasn't the same. It seemed different even though I couldn't pinpoint the difference. But why was it different? I looked inward as I had always done. Parental-induced guilt made that always the first resort for answers. Yet there were no answers that made sense. Just occasional glimpses of WHY.

I remember our time together at the next annual convention of the American Association of Law Schools. It was in New Orleans in early January. New Orleans was a popular and frequent convention choice for the AALS. Early January, warmth, bowl games, and twenty-four-hour festivity. Plus great food and music. Roger was in charge of restaurant selection as always, and after supper, he was leading a tour of bars and music venues. Some of us had had much too much to eat and drink. But Roger was still strong and leading the charge down Bourbon Street while singing along with any tune heard from nearby. Bill Summer, who had arrived at Eliot about the same time as Roger, was with us. His balance was compromised, his face reddened, and his speech slurred. But at one point he stopped, stood up straight to reach his hunched over 5'4", and shouted with clarity: "Roger, I have known you forever. This is the first time I have seen you let yourself go, the first time I have seen you without your shield and protective armor."

Roger then abruptly stopped singing and marching and immediately straightened to his full 6'4". He paused for a moment at attention. A marine officer in full command ready to inspect or review. He then took one giant towering step towards Bill, glared at him, and shouted: "Never ever!" And then Roger about-faced and left us and returned to our hotel. I was stunned, but Bill was not. He motioned to all as if to say "let's go drink, be merry, and enjoy great Dixieland."

The following morning, I found Bill at breakfast eating alone and asked if I could join him. He looked up and pulled out a chair for me to use. Bill appeared clear-headed and ready to lead a discussion at one of the convention seminars later that morning. After ordering my breakfast, I asked Bill: "Can you explain last night? You and Roger. What was that all about? What did you ask that got Roger so ticked-off? Were you surprised or is there some history I don't know?"

"Randy, there's no special history. Or mystery. It's the same for each of us on the faculty."

"Same what, Bill?"

"Randy, I'm surprised you haven't noticed. Roger is always in hiding, hiding himself from others. In a sense, we have never known the real Roger. He exposes nothing. He just refuses to say anything meaningful about himself or even his past. It's almost as if he speaks to us from behind a curtain of invisibility. We know Roger's vitae but not Roger. Conversely, he is always probing us and his students. He gets to the bottom of us without sharing. He has been my colleague, and a good one, for many years. But I can't say I know him. Randy, think about it. Play back your conversations since you arrived. Weren't you always the focus of serious conversations? I understand you visited his class. You observed how he functioned as a teacher. Isn't that the most you learned about him other than he was charming, eloquent, bright, and insightful?"

I thought long and hard about Bill's comments and my own experiences with Roger. I observed everything Bill described, yet I never really grasped it. From the very beginning, my private conversations with Roger focused on me. That's what I needed and wanted. Roger became my mentor as to everything I needed to know and think about and might have been hesitant to ask. He gave me direction and advice as a teacher and saved me from failure as a scholar. This seemed more than enough for a friendship, but was it beyond the present. Bill was his peer, his age, and his colleague of many years. Bill was an open book who didn't want a friend that remained closed. Yet why should this have mattered to me then or now as I put to words "my favorite colleague"? Do I really want more from Roger, information that could enlighten or burden? The genie is in the bottle, do I really need or want it to come out? I couldn't answer these questions, and I certainly didn't wish to agonize over them. So I left the matter alone with a friendship to play out as meant to be.

The following spring, Roger and I drove down to St. Louis for a Cardinal baseball game. A new ballpark, a beautiful evening in early May, and two tickets directly behind home plate but in the upper deck with a steep descent to first row seats and a perfect view of everything. What better way for two baseball fans to have a great time? We arrived early, got some hot dogs, beer, and peanuts, and settled in to watch a good game. Roger, an old Yankee fan from childhood, had become a Cardinal fan because of proximity. But I could not help but root for my childhood team, the visiting Cubs. The game was close, nothing to nothing, until the seventh when the Cardinals erupted with five runs. I turned to Roger with each run-scoring hit, and for the first time, I saw something different about Roger. The noise was deafening and the stadium shook. No smile, no exuberance, not even satisfaction, as his face lost all color and turned pale. "Roger, what's wrong."

"Randy, I've got to get out of here. Now! Before I pass out."

We left immediately and made our way to my car. Roger was unsteady throughout but refused any assistance. Within fifteen minutes, we were at my car. By now Roger was sweating profusely as his pale face turned to red. "Roger, where to? You need attention."

"Randy, back to Eliot City, it's only an hour's drive. University Hospital. They know me, I've been there many times."

"Roger, I don't want you passing out on my watch; I don't think this can wait an hour's time."

"Randy, trust me, I have been through this many times." The hour's drive frightened the hell out of me as Roger's condition worsened, with every breath labored. When we arrived at University Hospital, Roger went directly to the Emergency Room, asked me to wait, and then instructed me to call his wife to explain and tell her he would be home in two hours. I then waited, not understanding what happened and what came next. Two hours later, Roger was released and ready to be driven home. As he left my car, I noticed that he was neither pale nor red, no longer soaked in sweat, and was breathing comfortably. He said goodbye, thanked me, then made his way to the front door, and waved as he returned home at 1:00 A.M.

When I arrived home moments later, Berke was sound asleep. But she heard me, looked at the clock, and asked: "Randy, what happened?"

"Berke, I don't know. I can describe what happened, Roger had some kind of attack. Yet I don't understand; he did not explain."

Nor did he explain the next day or the next. Not then. I felt I could not talk about this with others, not even with those who knew him well or for a long time. Roger implied this episode was one of many. But still it could have been a well-kept secret. Roger also seemed to keep his distance. I did get to see him at the weekly lunches he led. But the one-on-one coffees that we often enjoyed after these lunches abruptly ended. Ended, until a month later, when Roger asked to have coffee with me late one afternoon. We met in his office and Roger wasted no time. "Randy, I owe you an explanation which I trust you to keep confidential." And with that I was given permission to witness a part of Roger seldom seen.

"Randy, I know you have heard that I was a marine during World War II, but not much more. Yes, I did serve in the South Pacific. My first and only invasion was a big one, Iwo Jima. It was towards the end of the War, and began on February, 19th of 1945. First wave, first to hit the beach, and first to be slaughtered. I was young, enlisted, optimistic, and destined for heroics. And I was determined to be brave, but bravery is elusive. It is never without fear, only a fool is without fear. It's just that the brave are never paralyzed by fear, at least not while in the eye of the storm. But what about after the storm? Are those that suffer the scars of storms—scars that destroy or paralyze—truly the brave and heroic? Perhaps it is only those that suffer the ultimate costs of bravery who qualify—those that stare down death and lose. I was among the first to scale Mt. Suribachi. I did not raise the flag, nor did I see it, but I did know one who raised it but never lived to see his family. I made it up the mountain, one of several in my platoon, but by the time victory was achieved a month later, I was the only survivor. I saw action from day one to almost the day we shipped out. A superficial gunshot wound did not stop me. I was determined to survive, although certain I would not. Letters home were filled with dread and goodbyes of every shape and form. The Japanese were everywhere, yet nowhere to be seen. Dug into the mountain in caves and tunnels. Some in my platoon simply disappeared at night, undoubtedly captured and dragged back into the hole from which their captors had emerged. Others had their throats cut after fatigue had taken them to that uncertain state between sleep and awareness. I never slept or at least recall moments of nothingness. Yet I made it through the month long battle. But a part of me did not. Once aboard ship, I broke down, and that part of me has never recovered. They would now call it post-traumatic stress. Some talk therapy, sedatives, and proclamations of 'you'll get over it' was all that I received. Randy, what you witnessed the other night has been with me ever since. Nearly always unpredictable, but most commonly in airplanes and driving at high speeds on busy highways. Sometimes in crowds like the other night. But I love baseball, and I thought I was beyond anxiety attacks when having a good time. I guess not. And that's it."

I listened, but didn't know what to do or say once Roger had ended his explanation. Roger rose from his chair and walked towards me as if to say "this conversation has concluded." As he went to open the door and usher me out, I extended my arms towards Roger to give him a hug. Roger was startled and immediately backed off and stood tall, towering above me as he might have in his past life as a marine officer. He had said too much and exposed too much of himself. Roger was for a moment not in command of the event or himself. He was vulnerable, and however he felt about his own vulnerability, others were never to witness it. And I was both witness to the event and explanation. As to friendship I could not help but feel something had been gained and then lost.

World War II was a real war for everyone around me, but especially for a teenager coming of age and anticipating entering the fight. Everyone was affected by it. Fathers, uncles, and brothers in Europe and the South Pacific. Most came back and most intact. And many not. Some on either coast knew air raid wardens, air raid warnings, and even blackouts. All knew rationing, bond drives, and old newspaper collections. And all knew war movies and especially Movietone news, which was for me far better than the Saturday afternoon double feature. We did not have TV or instantaneous coverage of any kind. We were not actual witness to the live events of each day, but we did have Movietone news and vivid enough beach landings and jungle fighting of the South Pacific. And we did have fear and clear recognition that this was a battle for something big. There was a strong sense of life-threatening danger to us as families because of loved ones away and at risk, and to us collectively because of our way of life under attack. And we didn't know how it would end, at least at the beginning with the news of Germany's march across Europe, the fall of France, the blitz of London, the bombing of Pearl Harbor, and the fall of Corregidor and the Bataan death march. As patriots, we were united and determined, but even that could not suspend reality and uncertainty.

And for me, there were maps of the South Pacific with blown up versions of major islands that had been lost and ultimately regained with bloody invasions and extended battles for control. I posted pins and notes of each victory that tracked the push back across the South Pacific to Iwo Jima and ultimately Okinawa. And I anticipated the celebration of the invasion of mainland Japan that never was because of a bombing raid made possible by a bomb never before seen which could never have happened without the successful invasion of Iwo Jima and Roger Davis and thousands of G.I.s like him. Roger had given me witness to something secret, and I wanted more. But not out of immediate concern for Roger. It was almost as if I had been pulled back to high school and teenage fascination. I remember my mother's first cousin, Robert Jay, stopped over night at our house while on his way home to New York at war's end. A marine and veteran of Guadalcanal and other major invasions. A survivor. My questions at supper made it impossible to enjoy a home cooked meal and, at midnight, impossible to sleep. Robert's entire overnight visit was unhappy for him and a disappointment to me. He left the next morning without ever acknowledging one of my questions. In leaving early before others were up, he thanked my mother and said: "Few people understand returning G.I.s, especially your son. War is not glamorous. It's not a board game for those under fire. It's real death and destruction and the loss of innocence, limbs, and best friends. Leave us be."

Over the years this simple "leave us be" has echoed from others I have known. Holocaust survivors have told me they never discussed their survival with children, grandchildren, and often spouses. Some children have added that their parents did not even disclose their real names and real past until near death. And occasionally, it was never. And it's been much the same from children I have known of returning G.I.s of World War II, Korea, and Viet Nam. (And probably the same for veterans of Iraq and Afghanistan.) Silence was the only way of coping and comfort. That was the way it was for Roger until the panic attack and disclosure. And that was the way it was thereafter. Never again did he discuss it, and never did I ask. Nevertheless, Roger did unveil again. Gradually and perceptibly was I able to glimpse the person seldom seen.

For many years, our friendship was a constant, especially in substance. He continued to lead interested faculty to lunch several times a week. But it was never quite the same, as the faculty tripled in size and cliques and factions took shape. The faculty's oneness eroded, especially in commitment to teaching and accessibility. Inevitably there were colleagues we did not know and some we did not care to know. Roger himself bridged many groups within the faculty, so his dance card at lunch was usually filled. On the days I joined him, there was always coffee afterwards, something that became obligatory over time. Roger continued to read and comment on everything I wrote, including multiple drafts of the same article. But we also discussed teaching. We agreed on much. And over the years, there were some subtle changes, especially as he listened and learned from me as I had from him.

As Roger approached mandatory retirement at age seventy, his health declined. At first, his knees gave out, and his commitment to fitness and exercise became irregular. Two knee replacements did not change anything as his condition and conditioning were only made worse by infection and pneumonia. But he did recover enough to continue teaching. In the classroom, he never again stood tall at well over six feet and on the move for an entire class hour while relentlessly moving up and down aisles and getting as close as possible to the student under fire. Never again did he resemble the marine sergeant he once was. All of this he shared with me, while confiding that he was now nailed to a chair behind a teaching desk and unable to use a chalk board because of compromised balance and stability. Roger knew that he had become a softer version of the "bear" he had once been, and he didn't like it.

During his last year of teaching, I asked Roger whether he would continue after retirement teaching a course or two at Eliot or as a visitor elsewhere. He immediately responded: "Randy, no, I will be finished with teaching when I finish my last class of the school year. That will be it, that's all there is." And then Roger paused as if he were waiting for my WHY. But he responded before I dared ask it. "Randy, I am not the same teacher, nor the teacher I want to be or must be. My teaching evaluations have held up just fine and are as good as ever. And once in a while, they are better than ever and even the best on the faculty. Yet the students don't know what I know. I am not the same. I am not as quick or as nimble and creative with answers and, most importantly, with hypothetical questions that move the student and the class up and down the mountain trail to insight, analysis, and understanding. Again and again, I must reach back into my quiver of questions from the past and recycle them. They suffice, or so it seems to everyone but me. But I know the freshness of what the student has said and where he or she has taken me. And I know the subtle differences that exist and the importance of new and original questions that slice the issues that exist with razor thin precision for me regardless of whether others perceive them or not. I KNOW. That hurts. It's the final blow signaling irrevocable loss. And Randy, I don't want to be in charge of a classroom when the students themselves know."

All I could say in response was "neither would I." And then Roger changed the subject, perhaps recognizing that he had shared much more than he intended.

After retirement, Roger came into school every day, sometimes to work on his own articles he seldom finished. Always he seemed more interested in the work of others, especially mine, as I continued to depend upon him for the most thorough and helpful edits I had ever seen. But over time, his comments seemed less and less instead of page after endless page of anything and everything he deemed helpful. Finally came his last edit: "Randy, good job, well done, I really liked it." During his early years of retirement, he also came into school to mentor new teachers and even old faculty friends, and sometimes merely to lead the lunch groups several times weekly. I would see him occasionally at lunch, but often at coffee. Roger would ask about me, and I would respond with a response that would become the subject of the entire coffee time. And sometimes I would ask about him with a preemptive question. Roger would seldom deflect. He didn't like aging and losses both physical and mental for him and his wife Lois. He complained, sometimes bitterly, with vents of great anger and sometimes with resignation. But sometimes he would, with subtlety and inevitability, focus on loss of identity in the institution he had served and loved for his entire professional lifetime. Two years after retirement, Roger couldn't help noticing that he was a daily stranger to all students. Not one recognized him or even cared to recognize the legendary teacher who once was. And several years later, this included faculty members, at least the young ones who cared little about the old and the past.

Then about five years into retirement, Roger shared news of his collision with mortality. He had been diagnosed with Parkinson's about two years earlier, and now it had become visible to others and had begun to advance rapidly. Roger soon lost confidence in many things, even those not directly attributable to the disease. He didn't want people to see what he had become, especially after he seemed to lose control over his body and sense of self. Roger's visits to the law school were rare once he ceased driving, and so were weekly lunches with faculty friends. But he did accept calls from me and invitations for lunch or just coffee. And once for a baseball game that was panic free. Or he would call and simply invite himself. And soon he would request help with something at home or call hoping to connect, preferably in person. I couldn't help notice each time how his Parkinson's had exposed his emotions, probably feelings always there but sealed tightly within. When I brought Roger home after an outing and as we said our goodbyes, Roger always allowed me to hold his arm, open the door to his home, and get him settled comfortably in his favorite chair. And then he would look me straight in the eye and thank me as his eyes reddened sometimes with tears of more than a few. Each time I would reach out to hug him and, unlike the time in his office when he revealed his story of war and survival, he would reach back and hug and not want to let go.

Roger had been known as the "Bear," a term never intended as one of endearment. But now he had morphed into a teddy bear, no longer the threatening grizzly. And I had become privy to his emergent sweetness and love of people. I will never forget what he said to me when confined to his home not long before death. "Randy, I know what I am today. I know what I like about me and what I don't. I can't stand the immobility and the helplessness that accompanies it, and I know it will never get better. I remember my towering strength and athleticism and I mourn. Yet at the same time, my emotions are now up front, witnessed by me and others. Randy, I don't have many regrets but one. I wish I had been more open, especially with those I care for. I never really made it with student friendships. Deep down, I think I would have been better off with at least some. Students respected me and, at least over time, fully appreciated my teaching and what they accomplished because of it. Yet these weren't friendships, something more than arm's length relationships. They thought they knew ME, but they really never did. And I thought I knew them, but I never could without their knowing me, or at least a little glimpse of me. I only wish that I could have shared then as I do now with you, and especially Lois, my daughters and grandchildren." And then he changed the subject and retreated back to the past and discussion of me. That was the last time I saw him.

When Roger's family had gathered in Eliot City following his death, I went over to Roger's home to visit with Lois and their family. They were cordial and hospitable and said they knew much about our friendship over many years. But I discovered they didn't know everything. Lois took me aside to show me what she had discovered in a small box among Roger's things. Three purple hearts from his time as a marine. She was unaware. Lois and her children couldn't help but have witnessed some of Roger's moments of panic and break-down. They surely saw him suffer, and she then said as much. But she never sought explanations, knowing he would stonewall until ready. She knew him well. He was never ready through the moment of death. Lois added: "Randy, the purple hearts give me a clue but not the understanding and appreciation I need. Do you know anything?" I could not lie and did not think Roger would have wanted me to. So I told her and his family everything Roger told me about Iwo and its aftermath. She listened carefully and then asked me to repeat every-thing as she needed to absorb it word by word. And then Lois broke down in tears and retreated to their bedroom. I soon left.

After Roger's death, the school held a memorial service and hundreds at-tended to remember. Colleagues, deans, staff, and hundreds of his students. There were six speakers, including me and three former students, along with many more that wanted to speak. Especially his former students. All thought they knew Roger and all came to love Roger because of what he gave to them. His teaching was viewed as tough love, yet masterful teaching that changed their lives forever. As I listened to his students I wished that Roger had been present. If only he knew, he may have approached death without profound re-gret. The service concluded with a video retrospect that marked important events in Roger's career, with his military experience barely mentioned. A high point was the video's accompanying music. "The Leader of the Band," composed and sung by Dan Fogelberg. Even after the visuals ended, the music continued as everyone sat silent in appreciation of our leader of the band.

In recent years, I have replayed in my mind many of the events of my friend-ship with Roger, and the one thing that nags at me, especially as I remember Lois and her not knowing about Iwo and Roger until I became the post-mortem messenger, is why me? Why me? A question Lois has undoubtedly asked as well. Perhaps he explained everything that fateful day in his office after that fated breakdown in St. Louis to silence me from asking questions of him or, worse, of others. He must have known that once I became the repository of truth that my sense of obligation would seal my lips. And it accomplished exactly that until after his death. Or was it simply his need to share, something long in coming, sharing made easier and necessary by the panic I had witnessed? Yet why not shared ultimately with the people closest and most important to him? Perhaps it was inertia at first and paralysis that inertia becomes over time, and finally the effort and toll that explanation requires of one ravaged by Parkinson's. Quite simply, maybe he had waited too long. I would like to have known, yet I will never know.

CHAPTER 4

RACE AND THE EDUCATION
OF A YOUNG TEACHER

E. Randall Mann

I will never forget the summer of 1969. Others of age or even coming of age would surely feel the same way. There was Viet Nam and protests. And Civil Rights movements and demonstrations in pursuit of equality for Blacks, a self-selected label that had supplanted Negroes as the term of respect and also power. The focus of both was often college campuses, and this included Eliot University. Spring was especially an active time with daily happenings that sometimes included sit-ins in administrative offices and buildings. Viet Nam and the draft were realities especially for men in graduate schools who often had to trade campus demonstrations and protests for six months of active duty in the National Guard or two years in the battle fields of Nam. No one, however, went untouched. Not students, not teachers, and not administrators. And beyond the campuses, cities sometimes burned while Blacks were bloodied, or worse, in pursuit of basic rights that others assumed and deemed inalienable. Yet for me, the summer of 1969 was mainly peaceful and very special. I was much too old for the draft but still young enough to experience and appreciate my most important educational moment.

In late February 1969, it all began with a visit to my office from Associate Dean Lou Robbin who knocked on my door unannounced. "Randy, I have an offer that you can refuse, but want you to accept. And I think you will regret a refusal and forever be thankful for an acceptance."

"Lou, it seems like you're trying to sell me the Brooklyn Bridge."

"No, Randy, this is not a scam. It's for real. Have you ever heard of CLEO?"

"Yes, but I don't know much about the program other than it's new."

Lou then began to explain. "CLEO is the acronym for Council on Legal Education Opportunity. In 1968, CLEO was founded as a non-profit project of the American Bar Association Fund for Justice and Education to expand opportunities for minority and low-income students to attend law school. This summer, the Eliot School of Law has agreed to host a Pre-Law Summer Institute for seniors or college graduates who plan to attend law school in the fall. Most have already been admitted to a law school, but some have not. Those who have not been admitted hope to use success in this program to gain admission somewhere. Some who have been admitted hope to use this program to upgrade their admission elsewhere. And all hope to use this summer experience as a Head Start on their legal education. Enrollment is limited, and each course will be taught in two sections. Both sections will be small, fifteen students in each. Four people will be teaching, three from other schools, and the dean and I would like you to represent us and become the fourth. Each will be teaching a first year required course, but only for six weeks which is the duration of the program. One course will be Civil Procedure, another will be Legal Writing, and the other two will be standard substantive courses. And I am asking you to teach your course on Property. The focus is upon writing and analytical skills, which means frequent tests and short papers along with conferences and significant feedback. And I am offering you one-fourth of next year's salary, $5,000.00, even though one course for six weeks is less than one fourth of your teaching load."

I then raised several questions and asked for more information. After responding fully, Lou asked for my decision. I told him I needed to discuss this with Berke at home and that I would have an answer the next day. That night Berke immediately replied: "Go for it. We can take an abbreviated family trip afterwards, and the $5,000 will mean we can afford a second car, and I have one in mind." So the next day I told Lou that my answer was yes and that I would be good to go when the program commenced.

The program began the first weekend of June with a reception for students and teachers. Lou was in charge and delivered opening remarks that addressed the goals, mechanics, and details of the program that covered just about everything. After introducing the faculty, food was served, and it was then time for mixing and engagement. I was never good at mixing and small talk, and then moving on to others to meet and greet. I was better at one-on-one. I was then and especially now. I never felt that unease in classes large or small. Dialogue in class always began one-on-one. And even though participation usually spread, I always focused on students individually, one at a time, and I could linger and stay individually in hope of achieving progress and meaningful experiences for each student. But I could never do this in a meet and greet. I could pontificate and hope to say things important, but it was never the same. Students would congregate, and individuals became a blur along with their names. Names were always my immediate objective in the first days of any course. I wanted to know each of the players as quickly as possible and hoped to abandon my seating chart at the end of one week, maybe two. And so the meet and greet became an opportunity to nail down some names with faces. Afterwards, I was disappointed that the number I had retained was less than ten.

Classes began on Monday, two sections daily, Monday through Thursday. Additionally, Thursday and Friday were days for weekly one-on-one conferences to discuss exams and papers. By the end of the first week I had imprinted the names of all thirty students in my memory and had accomplished my first goal. Yet there was much more to be learned. The class tone and interaction were different. In a section of merely fifteen students there was a dynamic I had never witnessed or encouraged. Two days of formal interactive discussion (in which students did not speak unless called upon or acknowledged when their hands were raised) was followed by spontaneous interruptions and interaction. My first reaction was pleasure and approval because it might have reflected uninhibited participation. But soon I recognized I had to take control. Unrestrained participation was an invitation to those who liked to dominate or simply hear themselves talk, and inevitably this behavior discouraged participation especially among the quiet and reticent. And I had seen the downside of this many times before. Yet in taking control, I had to set ground rules delicately to avoid inhibition and killing natural enthusiasm and excitement.

Within a week, I had called on everyone and gotten them involved. Everyone except one. Actually, I am not certain of his name. It's been many years since the summer of 1969, and I am a bit fuzzy as to names from the past, even the important ones. I tend to remember last names best. It's the way I call on students. "Mr. (.....) or Ms. (.....), would you please tell us about the case of *Alexander v. Alexander*." But for this student, I do not recall his last name; strangely, I seem to recall only his first name. Josh. I called on Josh midweek and was greeted with silence. I waited. More silence. "Josh, I will repeat the question." And I did. More silence. I then said something I had always announced to classes at the Eliot School of Law. "It's imperative that we all participate. The classroom experience is a collaborative endeavor in which your participation is as important as mine. Although I may lead and orchestrate, the analytical skill set needed to do the work of lawyers—essentially problem solving—is achieved primarily through your efforts. Not mine. This learning experience is active not passive, and we can't rely on a few to do the work required of all. And one more thing. I am not your antagonist. My questions are intended to assist, not obstruct, and certainly not to savage or destroy. If you are having difficulty, just give me something to work with, and then listen carefully to the next question, and then the next, and then the next. And I implore you to do this with patience. Now then, Josh, how about taking a chance?" No response, just painful silence. And I knew I had to move on to others and speak to Josh outside of class.

I waited until the end of the week until his scheduled conference time on Friday. On Wednesday, both sections had taken their first exam, and on Thursday afternoon and Friday, I was holding conferences for everyone. Josh was given a time slot for late Friday afternoon with no one to follow just in case his conference needed more time. I had read his written answers carefully, and read them again. They were outstanding, among the three best in the program, and among the best I had seen in my entire time teaching. Josh's paper identified the critical issue, carefully explained why it was the issue, discussed relevant principles of law, and then applied these principles to the issue in light of existing facts. Just as important, it was beautifully written with great clarity and organization. I was very impressed and also excited to meet with him in hope that this success would get Josh beyond initial stage fright in the classroom. But I was wrong. At 5:00 he did not show, so I waited for thirty minutes and then left. At first, I was disappointed, but that disappointment morphed into anger. Instinctively I had shifted from attempted understanding to retribution, and I knew that retribution seldom accomplishes anything, especially in teaching. I had to reach out again and simply make it work. Before leaving school for the weekend, I left a note for Josh.

Dear Josh:

I really need to see you. These conferences are required by the CLEO Program. Please meet me in my office this coming Monday at 5:00.

Sincerely,

Professor Mann

P.S. Your performance on the first examination was excellent.

On Monday, immediately after class, I was approached by Wilson Anderson, who was a student in the Program and a member of Josh's section. Wilson was an easy name and person to recall then and even today. He was outgoing, friendly, and smiled a lot within and beyond the classroom, and more importantly, Wilson was proactive with respect to questions and concerns. As a teacher, I was always accessible beyond formal conferences, and Wilson was in my office frequently. And for several years thereafter, he even sent me Christmas cards. But this time, Wilson's visit was not about him. "Professor, can I speak with you about Josh; it's important."

"Of course, let's go up to my office."

Once there, we sat down together at my round conference table. Mr. Anderson quickly began. "Professor, I have never done this before. Josh and I know each other from home. We are both from Philadelphia, Mississippi. I assume you have heard about Philadelphia."

"I certainly have, and how can one forget Philadelphia and the names of the three civil rights workers who were killed. Michael Schwermer. Andrew Goodman. James Chaney."

"My growing up and Josh's were the same. Same segregated schooling. Same teachers. Same poverty. But there were some important differences. Both of my parents worked for a well-connected and powerful white member of the community. His name was Elijah Jones. Essentially both my parents were servants for Elijah Jones and his family. My mother cooked, cared for his children, and washed and mended clothing. My father was a butler, but even more important, he could build and repair anything. And he did, always making things almost new again. Both were kept and protected from dangerous forces. No one would dare mess with Elijah Jones's Blacks. And my parents, my sister, and I knew how to avoid trouble. My sister and I grew up knowing we could never give our parents problems, reason to worry, and reason to beg Mr. Jones for anything. But Josh's family was different. Not Josh, but his father and his two older brothers. They were smart and everyone knew it, especially the Sheriff and his entire force. Worst of all, his father and brothers were plain uppity, forever asserting rights as if they were white men. His brothers weren't troublemakers, but they did trouble the community. They weren't shiftless unemployed alcoholics in constant violation of the law. Instead, they used the law to register voters, and lots of them. Josh, however, was quiet and always seemed to stay out of sight, especially when there was trouble. Actually, he was never seen, but never out of sight. Josh witnessed some awful things. I didn't know this then, but he saw his two brothers beaten and hung by their necks to die. Not long thereafter, his father died of natural causes, so they say. Heartache. But the Blacks of Philadelphia think otherwise. Professor, Josh is plain scared to death of you. Not just you, but all white men. White men until he came here were the Sheriff and his cronies. That's all he knew. College was a Negro college with no White teachers or students. White men are synonymous with the Sheriff and men with hoods. That's all he has known. And that's what he sees and fears in you, and he can't seem to get beyond it."

I never expected this explanation, and didn't know what to say. After three or four uncomfortable moments, I asked the obvious. "Will Josh meet with me today at 5:00 as I requested?"

"Professor, not without me. He does know that I have talked with you, but that doesn't diminish his fear. However, I think my presence may promote some trust."

"Wilson, I will see you and Josh later today. Thanks."

At this point, I was confident that I could change things enough to gain Josh's trust and communicate one-on-one without need of anyone else. My responsibilities as a teacher required intervention; after all, the practice of law required communication and interaction with clients, lawyers, and judges, and some were destined to be white. Somehow his fear and distrust had to be confronted and overcome. And Josh could do so. Perhaps this was no different than advising law students what to wear when they appear in court. But I was dead wrong. Josh and Wilson appeared at my office at exactly 5:00. And both immediately seated themselves with me at my round conference table. Josh sat with his head down, never looking up or at me. I began by reviewing what Wilson had told me and asked Josh whether there is anything that needed to be added or corrected. He shook his head NO. Next, I reviewed his examination answer carefully and thoroughly and explained why it was outstanding. And then I mentioned that, thus far, this exam performance is a clear indication of his talent for the law and what lawyers do. And then I said impulsively: "Josh, your next exam is Wednesday, two days from now, and conferences will be scheduled for Thursday and Friday. Let's have your conference over lunch, just you and me. I hope you like barbecue because Grandpappy's Barbecue is the best. How about it?"

Josh shook his head NO as he continued to stare at the floor.

"But Josh why not?"

And then I heard his voice for the first time. A deep voice, almost inaudible, and a presence enhanced by his height and two hundred fifty pounds or more. Josh's words were deliberate and bore the accent of the Deep South, and they were uttered without eye contact. "Professor, it's because I fear you'll tell me threatening things that you wouldn't if there were a third person to witness our conversation."

"But Josh it's me, not the Sheriff back home."

"Professor, but you're white, and I can never know you well enough to trust you. I have said too much. Can I leave now, please?" This time I responded silently by nodding YES.

I sat in my office deeply disappointed. I wondered why did I fail? Because I could not imagine what it was like to be Black in the deep South and experience Jim Crow and worse? But then I remembered something from childhood that should have been my compass at the outset. The year was 1940, and I was age ten and suffering from chronic asthma attacks. At that time, there were no steroids or albuterol inhalers. Nothing except a bathroom sink, hot water, a towel overhead, and steam. I will never forget the relief afforded by steam. Never long term, yet always long enough to yield peaceful slumber. But my mother had discovered a miracle doctor in Gulfport, Mississippi, who had developed an elixir which, if taken daily, could minimize the frequency and magnitude of asthma attacks. So she scheduled an appointment for me, and off I went with my father to Gulfport, first by train to New Orleans and then by bus along the Gulf to Gulfport. The moment I descended from the train onto the platform, I absolutely knew things were different. Colored only, Whites only. Toilets and water fountains. I had read and heard about slavery and segregation, but to witness the latter was different. Neither books nor movies are reality. Seeing it live and in the present is. I immediately knew I was in a different world. The same country but a different world. We continued our journey by Greyhound bus. My father sat down towards the front. And I sat next to him, though not for long. My favorite bus ride was always on the bench seat all the way in the back. My favorite because of the bumps that could send a small child into a series of exciting bounces; although never to the ceiling, it often seemed like it. (All long before seat belts.) This bus also had curtains. So that's where I went to enjoy the ride. I pulled back the curtains and sat down to enjoy the uneven surface of the four lane highway and the view of the Gulf. And then I saw the woman sitting on the same seat all the way to the other side near the window who was cringing with terror all over her face. Moments later the bus driver spied me in the rear view mirror and immediately stopped the bus on the shoulder of the highway. He then marched to the back, screamed at me, dragged me by the collar to my father, and ordered both of us off the bus. Once we were on the side of the highway, he closed the doors and gunned the engine. My father pounded on the door while I began to cry. Finally the driver opened the door, motioned us onto the bus, and shouted: "You god damn Yankees respect nothing. You just don't get it. You think you're better, but you ain't. Now sit down and behave and keep your damn mouth shut." But I guess even an experience like this could never be compass enough to comprehend the terror that Josh had confronted all of his life, especially as a witness to the beating and hanging of two brothers.

Certain things in life are unimaginable. Events and experiences that create clubs no one ever wishes to join. People may say "I can imagine (or even know) what you have been through." But they can't. It's unimaginable. A child's death? Unimaginable. I know, I'm a member of that club. But what it's like to be Black and subject to official segregation, Jim Crow, Ku Klux Klan brutality, and police who stand by and watch or sometimes participate in mob brutality or killings? And even though I experienced the terror of the bus driver and the effects of Jim Crow, I had violated rules designed to protect me, a member of the white race, and my way of life and a system in which I was the beneficiary and not the victim. How could I possibly know and fully appreciate the paralyzing fear indelibly imbedded in Josh's psyche. How could I? I could not.

Yet I could not give up my effort to gain the trust of Josh. Trust was at the root of all good teaching and teachers. It was at the core of positive chemistry that opened up minds to things new and challenging and liberated students to take chances without paralyzing fear of embarrassment or failure. It was the gold standard for student goodwill and favorable evaluations. It was an intangible coveted by all committed members of the academy. Josh was a challenge I might never overcome. Yet there was still some good news emerging. Actually it was very good news that could not have happened without a measure of trust. The dynamic was different. It was special. Each day was something new that was exciting and exhilarating. I was learning. I was becoming a better teacher. These Black students were in a program synonymous with affirmative action. Many would not otherwise have been admitted to quality law schools, and some not to any law school whatsoever. Mainly it was because of Law School Aptitude Test scores, tests that they had not been raised on and tests that some claimed failed to assess the true abilities of the disadvantaged. But my students clearly had what it takes to succeed. Mainly, these CLEO students were forcing me to rethink the obvious.

"Professor Mann, you ask us to state the issue, but you don't give us a methodology for arriving at the issue in every case."

And then I would explain the issue or issues in a particular hypothetical or case under consideration. "Now then, do you all understand?"

"Yes, Professor, we do understand once you explain. But how do we understand and do it ourselves BEFORE you explain? We always understand the answer once we have the answer, but how do we do it before the answer?"

This stopped me in my tracks. Each time I responded in the same manner with a new example and a new explanation. But in time I recognized that I was essentially saying something my teachers had said to me, something generations of teachers had said again and again. "Just follow along as we discuss case after case, example after example, and you'll eventually catch on. Somehow you will get it by osmosis." And I was bothered. I knew that was not enough, and should never be enough. So I began to experiment with strategies and methodologies that might give concrete guidance to identifying issues on their own. Ultimately, I settled on argumentation, what did the plaintiff argue step-by-step, and what did the defendant argue. And which propositions produced disagreement. This technique could direct students to primary and subsidiary issues. This was the first thing I learned, yet there were many more moments of insight and enlightenment that forced me to experiment and to develop new techniques for learning important skills. Most important for me, these experiences informed and enhanced my teaching at the Eliot School of Law. Methodologies from that summer all made their way into my Property course and, over the years, became important cornerstones for developing analytical skills.

Following my meeting on Monday with Wilson and Josh, the week went very fast with more classes, an exam, grading that exam, and conferences. Once again, Josh did very well, and once again his exam was among the very best. And once again, I scheduled him for my last conference on Friday at 5:00. This time Josh appeared promptly, not by himself but as expected with Wilson. I began by praising his exam performance and reviewed carefully and in detail what made it outstanding. I then observed some areas that could be improved but also noted that perfection is near impossible, especially with exams that include too much given the time constraints. I then asked Josh whether he had questions or anything else to discuss. He shook his head NO, again with his head down, and then stood up as if to leave. At that point I stood up as I tried to gain eye contact: "Josh, could you please sit down for just a moment, I have one question." We both sat down. "Josh, will you tell me how you learned to write so well. Was it at home? At school? Or on your own, perhaps by imitating writing styles you admired in books you had read? Your exam is well organized, clearly expressed, and very literate, especially if one considers the pressures of time on a law school exam."

His response was delayed as if he were asking himself whether to reply or what to say. But he did reply, as his head lifted up towards me, even though his eyes never found mine. "Professor, my parents and brothers were smart, very smart, but I did not learn to write at home. It was at school with Black students, Black teachers, and segregation. My English teachers. Every one of them, no matter the grade. They were the toughest and most demanding. No nonsense and no forgiveness. If you didn't master grammar and diagramming sentences, your knuckles were turned raw. They were products of separate but equal, but they were better than equal, they were superior." And then, without more, Josh stood up, looked at me as if he wanted permission to leave, and then left before I could respond.

The next week was essentially more of the same. Another exam and another excellent blue book from Josh. Once again, Josh and Wilson arrived for the last conference on Friday afternoon, and once again, I explained to Josh why his exam was among the best. But he had no questions and stood up to leave. Again, I asked him to stay for a moment, because I wanted to give them a heads-up on something I would assign specially for them during class on Monday. They both sat down as I saw customary student fear register in their eyes. "Gentlemen, I wish to experiment with something on Monday, something I have never tried. Throughout this course we have been focused on issues raised by a set of facts and how to arrive at them. Each of the cases presents a story and a set of facts that gives rise to conflict and litigation. And you are asked to identify the issues, the critical questions before a court, in light of principles of law you are learning from the decisions in these cases. This is the way in real life that lawyers discover issues, address them, and learn to resolve them. And it is also the order in which you must address an exam and demonstrate skills you have learned. Story and facts first, next relevant legal principles, and then issues. This is the context in which you identify issues and master them and the facility for addressing and solving real legal disputes. But I firmly believe one can enhance the process of learning these skills by reversing this order and observing the same interrelationship between facts and legal principles. Specifically, I think one can learn just as much by creating an exam question as well as by answering one. So on Monday, I will announce that all exams henceforth will be questions created by groups of students, and for the first week I am asking the two of you to create the exam question for the week, to grade the answers, and then to explain your answer to your own question to the class at the end of the week. And on Monday, I will meet you briefly and give you two principles of law that I want to be at the heart of the issues in the dispute you create. I want you to prepare a story and a conflict that raises issues with respect to only these two principles and their application. And I will explain further on Monday. Now that's all for today." They again stood up to leave. They looked stunned, something I anticipated.

On Monday, I met with Josh and Wilson after class to give them the two legal principles, and I elaborated further on what I expected them to prepare. Additionally, I presented an illustration of what I wanted them to do using two other principles, and then asked them to see me the next day with their exam question which the class would take on Friday. Again they were stunned, but Josh, at least, did not for a moment appear frightened. The next day after class, they appeared with a one page question which I quickly read. It was brilliant. I was expecting a question involving two transactions concerning a single tract of land, each raising issues respecting one of the two principles. But no, their question used a single transaction in which the second principle was spun off of a potential resolution of the first issue. So I told them I approved and gave them instructions on how to create a grade base they could use in grading fellow classmates on their exam answers, and that they should be ready to discuss everything on Monday in class. This time they appeared confident, not stunned.

Their exam was given on Friday, and on Monday they returned graded exam papers to every student in their section. Their discussion of the issues, application of the legal principles, and the grading process was thorough and excellent. But it all came from Wilson. Josh remained silent just the same as he had in previous classes. After class, I asked them to stop by briefly, so they followed me immediately back to my office. "Gentlemen, Wilson carried the load today exclusively. Was this assignment a joint venture or was it all Wilson? I think I know the answer, but I need to hear it from you."

"Professor, we divided things up. Essentially Josh drafted the question and the grade base, and I did the rest." I replied that I suspected that and sent them on their way. I shouldn't have been surprised, because of the sophistication of their question and the exceptional ability Josh had already displayed for a student at the very beginning of his legal education. If only he would speak up for all to glimpse the diamond shrouded in silence.

In the remaining weeks of the course, this wish was granted. Silence was broken, although trust was never achieved. The following week, in an effort to identify issues potentially before the court, we were attempting to reconstruct the arguments of the plaintiff and defendant in a particular case. Two students were struggling to accomplish this because of their inability to identify necessary steps and assertions in the formulation of the particular argument. So I simply asked: "Does anyone know what must come next in this argument?" No one raised their hand as I looked about and hoped. I did not like dead ends where I would have to answer my own question. I wanted desperately—always—to ask the right questions that gave direction to students to carry the inquiry and the class forward. But then I heard his voice, Josh's voice. No raised hand. Just his voice.

"Professor, I think I can help."

I was surprised to hear him volunteer, but not to witness his commanding presence and ability to construct an argument piece by piece. But apparently his classmates were surprised to hear him volunteer for something others could not do at that moment. Josh would not speak with me without the presence of Wilson, yet I had read his exams and knew the power of his intellect and the clarity with which he could express his ideas. His classmates were not privy to his exams and my appraisals. They simply did not know this side of Josh, although Wilson and I did. Josh was quiet and kept to himself, except for Wilson. And so they listened. In awe. Just as I did, even as I knew what I was about to behold. It was the perfect argument. And then Josh offered an alternative argument as well. Both presented with confidence, authority, and clarity. After Josh had finished, I wanted to follow up with questions that would enable him to explain his thought process in constructing his arguments and enable me to punctuate and affirm. Yet I did not dare. I did not want to risk silence or a non-response by Josh that would have detracted from and diminished what we had all just heard. So when Josh finished, I simply said, "WELL DONE." And I smiled as his classmates applauded.

The summer CLEO Program was coming to conclusion with the arrival of the last exam, the last class, and the last conference. Deep down I was hoping that Josh would attend his conference without need for Wilson. But both walked into my office at the appointed time. I began by reviewing all that Josh had demonstrated and accomplished in a short period of time, and that I firmly believed his potential as a law student and lawyer was exceptional. And then I added that if he ever needed a letter of recommendation that I would be pleased to provide one. I then asked whether he had any questions or anything else he might wish to discuss. Josh quickly replied NO as he rose to leave. I immediately raised my hand as if to stop him. "Josh, will you have a cup of coffee with me later today? Just the two of us?"

"Professor, no but thank you." Josh then moved closer to the door, but before he opened it, he turned to face me and said: "Professor, why can't you leave me alone? I really do appreciate all that you have taught me, discovered and affirmed in me, and all that you have offered on my behalf. But I don't want more even if I might need more. I am very uncomfortable with your presence even with Wilson at my side. You must understand the reasons for this extreme discomfort. It's part of my being and method of survival in the worst of times. It's who I am! Maybe not forever, but certainly for now. I know that my work and reach as a lawyer will be limited because of my inherent fear and distrust of the white world. If it continues, then so be it. But If I am to change and broaden my horizons, I can't rush the process. It is what it is, and I accept that." And then Josh opened the door and left along with Wilson.

It was the last time I saw Josh. I was at a loss. I had failed. I had failed even though that summer I had discovered something new sparked by student confusion and their questions that followed. Something new that led to innovated teaching techniques that were important and useful to Josh and his classmates and to many classes that followed at the Eliot School of Law. But still the experience didn't feel good. I was able to instruct Josh and impart the foundations of a skill set essential to the work of lawyers, but I couldn't reach Josh. I couldn't gain trust which I firmly believed was a cornerstone of effective teaching. I simply could not penetrate his protective shell borne out of history and the horrors of personal experience. My mood was soured through the end of the summer. But with a new school year and a new first year class, there was renewal, as there always was. And with this, there was a sense of excitement, especially because I was now loaded with fresh techniques that would enhance my ongoing experiments in learning. In time, I forgot about Josh. No, not really. Quite simply, he was no longer on my front burner, in my immediate consciousness, dominating my sense of responsibility, and governing my mood.

But I do think about that summer and Josh, especially now that I am retired over forty years later. And I do think about teaching and the importance of trust. Something essential to lawyering and, as well, to all of life. Even now, my experience with Josh disappoints and forces me inward. And I ask myself why as always. Why now, so many years later? Why now do I question this failure at trust when my success as a teacher proclaims it? I know what my wife Berke would say, my wife the realist philosopher. "Randy, get over it! You can't win them all. Life doesn't work that way. Not everyone will like you, perhaps respect you, but not like you enough to grant you trust. There will always be some who sit back in the shadows because they are without the trust sufficient to a leap into the unknown with you in class and beyond. Stop beating the dead horse; get off it. Randy, your preoccupation borders on personal arrogance. We all fail at something. Get over it." Personal arrogance, something I dislike in others and abhor in myself. Get over it! Especially now in retirement with no students to gain trust, get over it!

Yet in retirement, with the advances of the internet and search engines, I might now easily discover what the future held for Josh and even Wilson. If alive, I imagine I could find them. I assume both returned to Mississippi, which was dangerous for Blacks in 1969 and many years thereafter. Fear of White authority figures, especially police, would not disappear easily, if at all, even over four decades. But why not find out? I may discover that Josh had embraced trust rooted in his summer experience of 1969. Josh may even have achieved greatness. Or maybe not. Perhaps it was obscurity instead. Would pursuit of Josh be continued beating of the dead horse? Would this be an act of arrogance or mere curiosity? I want to believe it's the latter. But yet, do I want to know what's happened to Josh? Lawyers often say "those who can't do must teach." I am also familiar with a corollary: those who preach often can't do what they preach. And I have preached for years to students in distress that one must know one's self, know one's effort, know what one has learned and accomplished, and know one's value. This process of self-evaluation begins in law school, or before, and ultimately must be the critical barometer for personal success and satisfaction. And it is something self-sustaining that becomes preeminent, especially after one has reached the top with no more promotions, no more bosses in sight, and no more artificial mountains to climb. But can I live by what I preach?

CHAPTER 5

ALMOST A DEAN

E. Randall Mann

After all these years, I have not forgotten the details. It was a Monday in early September of 1970. I was returning from class to my office and stopped in the mailroom to check for mail and phone messages. This was before computers, the internet, e-mails, texts, tweets, and even voicemails; it was when messages were left with telephone operators and secretaries. And there it was, a message from Chancellor Dan Thomas's secretary. "Could you please meet with the chancellor and the provost in the chancellor's office this afternoon at 4:00? Please call asap to confirm." What was this about? I had no idea, as my thoughts turned to speculation searching for the worst scenarios, as was my nature, but knowing they were unrealistic if not absurd.

I knew both Dan Thomas and the Provost Martin Fainsod, but not well. Both preceded me as members of the faculty at Eliot University and had served as chancellor and provost for over fifteen years. They were popular, effective, and highly successful leaders of the university during its ascension and ultimate recognition as an elite institution. They shared a vision of what Eliot University could become and were instrumental in its march to achieve it. Both were very personable and seemed easy to know and like. And I did like both, yet I recognized that I hardly knew them. Although I had received a distinguished teaching award several years earlier at a university celebration and dinner, I thought they barely knew me or even of me. I had seen them at all kinds of university and law school functions, but our conversations always seemed formal to the point of stiff and distant. But still I liked them or at least fully appreciated what they had achieved on my behalf and on behalf of every member of the university community. Clearly I could not ignore their summons, and so I immediately called back to confirm.

I arrived fifteen minutes early and was immediately ushered into the chancellor's study that adjoined his main office. It contained a beautiful work desk, paintings and photos of the university commemorating his many years there, book shelves stacked full of books — well known and not — and three huge leather cushioned chairs perfect for discussions, interrogations, and even afternoon naps. His secretary then offered some tea or coffee, and I accepted the latter mainly because of mounting anxiety attributable to my unknowing. And I waited. Both the chancellor and provost arrived together fifteen minutes late. I stood up, shook hands, as we all sat down in unison. Dan was slight and short in stature but always regal and kindly in presence. He gave and commanded respect and no nonsense. After some back and forth efforts at proper cordiality, Dan Thomas then got to the point. "Randy, did you know that Will Leslie has resigned as dean of the law school effective January 1, 1971?"

"Dan, I knew he was contemplating another deanship offer, but I did not know he had reached a decision."

"Well he has decided, and an official announcement should be made by tomorrow or the next day. Do you have a reaction?"

"I am not sure what you mean or are expecting me to say."

With that, Martin Fainsod got to the point: "Randy, did you want him to stay?" Martin's reputation always preceded him. Cunning. Measured. Brilliant. Translation: tread carefully.

"Martin, that's a loaded question, and I don't know where this conversation is headed. Will Leslie arrived the year before I did. He hired me, and he's the only dean I have ever known. I have liked him and what he has accomplished. But not everything. All deans have their critics. For that matter so does every president, chancellor, or provost. It's inevitable, especially for those who stay a long time. You just can't satisfy everyone within an educational institution filled with prima donnas all of the time. PRIMA DONNAS. After all, that's what tenured professors are or at least become over time."

With that, the chancellor interrupted: "Let me cut to the chase. We will be announcing a major fundraising campaign in less than a year, and we need our deans in place beforehand. We do want to conduct a national search for the dean of the law school, but in discussing this with Martin, several alumni, and two of your colleagues at the law school, we believe the school already has the best choice on the faculty. Randy, your name comes up as the ideal choice with us and the constituencies we have canvassed. We still wish to conduct a national search with a committee, but you currently are more than a front-runner in a search that will be carried out expeditiously. I am asking you to apply. I am confident that you will not regret it."

I sat in silence, probably for less than a minute, but it seemed forever. As a lawyer and a teacher, I always tried to anticipate everything, first in the court-room and in planning, drafting, and implementing a business or estate plan, and thereafter in the classroom. As a teacher, over ten years of experience helped. A lot. But I still worked at it, devoting many hours to class preparation anticipating every twist and turn bright minds could take. Yet I never antici-pated the precise substance of this meeting and where it might lead. I could not remain silent much longer, and knew I had to say something however inept. "Dan, quite frankly, I did not anticipate the direction of this conver-sation, and certainly this moment. I am flattered and do appreciate your con-fidence in me. But I need to give this some thought and discuss it with my wife, Berke. Can we continue this discussion in two days, Wednesday?"

"Of course, but don't you have some questions for Martin and me at the moment?"

"I am certain that I do have questions, but for now I don't wish to waste your time, and besides I will have lots more on Wednesday."

"Randy, then how about adjourning until 4:00 P.M. on Wednesday?"

I nodded yes, excused myself and left to return to my office where I imme-diately called Berke and told her we needed time tonight to discuss at length an unexpected opportunity.

By the time I arrived at our house, our two children had returned from after school activities, were hungry and ready to have supper so that they could complete homework assignments. Before we sat down, Berke whispered "so what's this unexpected opportunity all about?"

I simply replied: "A deanship."

Berke's face and tone of voice, even with no more than a single word— "Oh"—could always say everything, and they did. And so I sat through and tried to enjoy a favorite meal and great conversation with our daughter and son expecting a red flag later in the evening. And a red flag it was, if not a NO, at least concern and caution. I began our conversation by relating every-thing that had occurred earlier in the day with the chancellor and the provost. Berke listened carefully, and when finished I nodded as if it were her turn to weigh in. "Randy, although I do not think you will like being a dean, I KNOW you will be a successful dean, especially here at Eliot University. And I know you would not begin the process by applying or accept the appointment without full commitment to making the deanship a success. But I also know that success requires my participation and commitment, especially with a university-wide fundraising campaign at the center of your tenure as dean. You will need me to entertain select alumni at home or elsewhere or to cohost school functions. And much more. The fact is that you are married, and this kind of position comes with certain expectations for spouses. Randy think about it, just how many unmarried deans do you know? Any? Any who have been successful? Probably not, and there's good reason. They need cohosts to fulfill expected roles that facilitate hospitality and goodwill, and neither secretaries nor administrators ever work. It takes a charming spouse. All of the deans's wives I have known have been stay-at-home spouses, and their husbands could not have done their jobs effectively without their contributions, undoubtedly both unpaid and unrecognized. Randy, success as a dean won't happen without sacrifices by me. Specifically my career path. We have become a two career marriage. That wasn't the expectation my parents or my generation held for me, nor was it your expectation either. You envisioned me as a career homemaker, and you did so despite the extraordinary professional career your mother pioneered as a lawyer and breadwinner. It may not have been even my expectation when we met and married. But it became mine, because I had a mind and abilities and talent to do much more, and I did not want to live a life of suffocation. So while you have established a distinguished career as a teacher over the last fifteen years, I have struggled to make a life in primary education as a teacher and author, and I have done this from scratch. And something has got to give for you to become a successful dean. Unfortunately, I know it must come from me, and I don't like it after all the time and effort to bootstrap a terrific career and a reputation that accompanies it. Damn it, I know where we are headed and I am frustrated. NO! I am downright angry."

As I look back, I recognize how different things were at that time as compared to now when I recall my moment as Almost a dean. The faculty was very small by comparison to today, fourteen then and sixty now. And there was no diversity: one woman and the rest men, and all Caucasian. Further, the student body was also small by comparison, eighty then and close to three hundred today. As for diversity, until the late 1960s, it was token with three or four women and the rest men. Among them one African-American, two Asians, and the rest Caucasian. By comparison, today's diversity is real. Close to fifty percent are women, fourteen percent are African-American, twenty five percent are Asian, Indian, and Middle Eastern, and the rest Caucasian. Most of all the problems deans had to confront and overcome were different. Life during the 1960s at the Eliot School of Law in many ways seemed easy. Faculty salaries were low and so was tuition. And between income from endowment and tuition, the school had an annual surplus that enabled its reserves to grow and grow. Enrollment was expanding, and new law schools were emerging with Baby Boomer demand on the horizon. Life seemed sweet and uncomplicated except for war and civil rights. As serious as the issues of frequent campus demonstrations and student unrest were because of Viet Nam, the draft, and the civil rights revolution, they did come to an end because of withdrawal from Viet Nam and significant changes in law that enlarged the rights and protections afforded to minorities, most prominently African-Americans. And for some unknown reason, I was confident that I would be good at handling student unrest, and in particular, the demands of law students for inclusion in decision-making directly affecting them.

Although this period of unrest was protracted and tumultuous, it was never as daunting as today's unending issues of costs, tuition, student debt, and the contraction of job opportunities for law students as firms large and small were merging, jettisoning partners and not hiring associates, or sometimes going belly-up. Today's dean has had to manage a fine line that includes cost reduction with the highest component being faculty salaries, increased income through new programs and major fund raising and, at the same time, maintain or improve the school's U.S. News ranking. And this has been a fine line that threatens the existence of many schools. Today's landscape has not been an easy one for the best of deans to manage. But it was not the landscape I had to confront in 1970. Nevertheless, Berke's concerns and conceptualization of her spousal role were prescient. She knew that a dean's wife had to be involved, even in good times, and that the University Wide Campaign required entertaining, hospitality, good feelings for all, and hard work. She felt that a dean could not simply stand by and ride the crest of a wave because down-times were inevitably ahead. And I knew she was absolutely correct.

I did not want our discussion to end because Berke was right. She had worked even harder at her career than I had, and she had accomplished this as a homemaker as well. Her career would suffer even if she could continue part-time. But I knew I needed her to be successful. I don't know why, but I blurted out the first thing that came to mind: "How about an appointment and salary from the school?"

Berke's reply was immediate and direct: "Randy, I wish it were otherwise. I wish our lives would continue as is, both of us respected teachers and authors, perhaps even well-known. And I am not certain why I should agree to something without more explanation. Why do you want to shake things up? Why change? Why a deanship that takes you away from things you like so much? Quite simply, you haven't explained. Please explain. Randy, talk to me and now!"

"Berke, I haven't explained, perhaps I can't adequately, at least not now. My first reaction to the chancellor's invitation was a sense of high regard and unforeseen importance. I was flattered beyond expectation. They practically guaranteed something accompanied by notability, power, and comparative wealth. It is an open door to leadership. How could I turn down this opportunity? It seemed like the logical next step in the career of a successful academic. And I thought this was enough introspection to move forward with my candidacy."

"Randy, personally, I don't think this is enough forethought. Again, I firmly believe you will be successful, but I also know you will be unhappy, maybe very unhappy. Nevertheless, although I am angry and frustrated, I won't stand in your way, grumble, and give you grief. But I won't support you and become your teammate except on two conditions. First, I need a truly reflective answer to my big question: if fame, fortune, and leadership are your only reasons for going forward, are they enough to replace all that you inevitably lose at work, like the joys of teaching and friendships with students, and sacrifices at home, like irreplaceable lost time with two children? And I know that I don't have to fill in the blanks on the extent of these losses. Second, I like the idea of an appointment and salary. A title is unnecessary, but an attractive salary is!"

Wednesday at 4:00 was upon me in a flash, but this time I was ready after a full day of anticipation and preparation. My meeting with the chancellor and provost lasted three hours, and we covered just about everything, mostly issues that I introduced, but many that they raised as well. The law school had already broken ground on a new building because of soaring applications reflecting a national trend in demand for legal education. This building had the capacity to accommodate a student body double our size, and there was a lead gift large enough for the building to bear the donor's name. After some discussion, Dan Thomas made clear that the University Wide Campaign would include gifts sufficient to expand the student body and support five additional tenure track positions for the faculty. And they did not flinch when I reviewed the increased costs that accompanied expansion, not the least of which was the library. They anticipated raising tuition, which had been stable for several years, and at the time I believed this increase was reasonable. Finally, I made the request concerning Berke after explaining how essential she was to my success and ultimately the deanship and the law school's role in the campaign. At that point, Dan took over. "Randy, this discussion concerns an invitation to apply for the deanship and not an actual offer. To be sure, there is a probability of the latter. Yet there is no offer on the table at the moment. Nevertheless, I think we will be able resolve your problem when we arrive at an offer and discussion of salary. I do agree that a dean's spouse has a vital role in the success of a deanship just the same as a chancellor's spouse. But I can't begin a discussion of salary specifics until I survey the market. As you know, we haven't had to hire a law school dean in some time." I then told Dan and Martin that I would apply for the job, and the meeting ended shortly thereafter.

At home that evening, I told Berke about the discussion, that I thought her salary request would be resolved through an increase in mine that would reach her each month directly or indirectly. Berke is, and has always been, a realist. She immediately said a position and independent salary would have been preferable, but the arrangement you project is what I expected and would suffice. She then said: "Now what about the big question and your motivation to be a dean? Fame and fortune only?"

"Berke, thus far I haven't given it much thought, yet I do know I might regret it if I don't begin the process. I do love teaching and its rewards along with the opportunity to research and write. But I don't ever want to experience burn-out. I dread it because I have seen it in others. You pushed me into teaching, for which I am forever grateful. It wasn't easy. It was filled with unknowing and fright, and you were a witness to everything, including some serious stumbles on the way to tenure. But I made it as a teacher and a scholar. I succeeded, and I did it with a positive reputation that always precedes me when I walk into the classroom. Getting there became something more than fear. It was exhilarating almost beyond explanation. And now—and now a part of me wishes I could do it all over again. Oh how I wish I could climb that mountain again and again in quest of self-validation and joyous exhilaration. But that mountain no longer exists, so maybe I'm really searching for another mountain, another challenge, and another professional high. Berke, for now that's all I have in my defense. For now, however, I think it's all I need to proceed. Applying for this job doesn't mean I can't back out of the process if I discover my reason is not reason enough. And you will always know what I am thinking throughout. I promise."

To all of this Berke simply replied: "Randy, I think you will discover this is not reason enough. Yet I am supportive, I am patient, and I strongly believe more insight is forthcoming." Thereafter, I kept Berke in the loop every step of the way in quest of this deanship, but I did not share further matters of insight and rationale until my moment of truth two months later.

The dean search began with the appointment of a committee consisting of several faculty members, two law school graduates, and the dean of the business school, who also served as the chair. There were fifteen people who applied, mainly faculty members from elsewhere; one was a former dean, and another was a colleague at Eliot. In addition, the applicants included a practicing lawyer and a retired judge, both graduates of Eliot. Fifteen people in all, fifteen Caucasian men. Each of us were then interviewed by the committee, with no more than five to be invited for return interviews by the faculty. The group of four chosen by the search committee included me, my colleague, and two law teachers from distinguished schools. These interviews began with a reception hosted by the chancellor and provost, which included a dinner and evening presentation by the candidate that focused on his vision for the school. The following day concentrated on interviews of the candidate by faculty members, in small groups and also individually, and all non-faculty members of the search committee were invited to participate in everything. The visit of each candidate concluded with interviews with the chancellor and provost. And following the visits of all four, the chair of the search committee was to gather faculty reactions to each of the four candidates. Thereafter, the committee was to meet, deliberate, and recommend three candidates to the chancellor for selection of the next dean of the law school.

I was the second candidate to present and interview, and having decided to enter the contest, I wanted to fulfill the expectations of the chancellor and succeed. So I prepared and prepared, especially as to hot issues and hot buttons among my colleagues. And I did not shrink away from controversy. I discussed matters of size, anticipated enrollment, budgets, fund raising, and alumni relations, including faculty responsibilities respecting the latter two. I discussed curriculum and the emergence and importance of clinical education. I discussed student relations, matters of patience, and preparation for more seasons of demonstrations. I emphasized the importance of being proactive and giving students an advisory role on committees directly affecting their interests. Above all, I stressed that I was opposed to stonewalling change, especially that which was inevitable and certainly that which advanced the quality and feasibility of legal education.

During my presentation I was very conscious of expressions within the room. I observed a measure of reticence, probably because my colleague-candidate was in the room for each of the presentations just the same as I would be, and no one wanted to offend. Nevertheless, I was able to pick up on frequent smiles and nods of approval, but also scowls of disapproval, as I touched on issues, directions, and policies that some embraced, and others bitterly opposed. And when it came time for questions, there were surprisingly few. Actually, they weren't really questions. Instead they were long-winded statements in support of what they thought I had said or implied. In each instance I found myself saying either thank you or adding a clarification to avoid misinterpretation. A few weeks later, after all interviews had been conducted and the search committee had concluded its deliberations, their three recommendations went to the chancellor, who said that he would make his selection within several weeks. And I learned I was among the three.

Despite Berke's admonition, I had stepped into the dean competition, and up to that point, I found myself wanting to compete. Long term reasons for pursuit of the job were pushed aside, but could never stay aside for long. Once in a while I would return to reasons, and once again summon up notability, power, prestige, wealth, leadership, and another glorious and exciting mountain to climb. Wasn't a deanship the next logical step of academic life? Assistant professor, associate professor, professor, chaired professor, dean, provost, chancellor? When I would think about it, that always seemed enough, yet I could never feel it, embrace it, and make it mine. Nevertheless, I plunged ahead knowing if I changed my mind for reasons other than because of the unsatisfactory details of an actual offer that I had to do it soon. Very soon, which meant before the chancellor completed his deliberations. Waiting too long risked ill will with a good man and perhaps my future at Eliot University. I had one week before a decision, perhaps two, perhaps several days. I did know that Martin Fainsod was involved in a major conference in England and that Dan would want to confer with him. Despite these calculations, I found myself still competing and fundamentally waiting for a decision and perhaps becoming a dean through procrastination and ultimately by default. And that made no sense to someone who tried to make sense of everything. But my hand was forced soon enough, not by Berke, not by an accelerated time table, but by my colleagues.

One day after the search committee made their three recommendations to the chancellor, Bill Summer, an elder statesman on the faculty, knocked on my office door, entered with a grim sense of urgency, and began speaking before I could even acknowledge his presence. It was not really a discussion or even a speech. More like a lecture of what to do and not to do as the obvious inchoate dean. The lecture seemed like coded remarks of self-protection against the forces that threatened his position and power on the faculty. But the more he lectured, the more he became un-coded. He openly favored things new that favored him or at least did not undermine his interests. And he ranted about things un-favored and the colleagues who favored the un-favored. He then declared with a raised voice: "You will have my full support because you will do the right things!" Bill was normally soft-spoken and understated. His sword was humor, almost never anger. But this time was different. He was over the top with expressions that matched his voice. Both spoke volumes. Yet Bill was not the only visitor with a message of personal importance. There were others like Ralph Livingston and Willy Greenfield. Both presented cases for merit-based salaries instead of standard raises in fixed amounts for all faculty members. But for Willy, merit meant scholarship production—measured by number of publications and their quality—and for Ralph it meant teaching—measured by the number of students enrolled in HIS classes and the quality of teaching in each. Neither was animated. Their remarks seemed casual but uttered with absolute certainty almost as if their expectations were an inevitable truth. A truth perhaps, though not self-evident to all, but surely made quite clear to me. As I look back, there were one or two others who caught me in the hallways and made certain I understood their interests and hoped I had their backs. But the most important message came several days later just as I was nearing my self-imposed deadline to forge ahead or withdraw from the competition. And it came from Roger Davis, my mentor from earliest years of teaching.

The knock on my office door was unmistakably his, loud in phrases of three and rhythmic. And so was his entry. Immediate. No need for an invitation. An unlocked door meant he was privileged to enter at will and find his place at my round table, which he did while beckoning me to join him. The subject was the issue of the moment without need of explanation, introduction, or niceties of the day. Once I was seated, Roger began. "Randy, don't do it. Get out and do it now before pride forces you to accept the inevitable offer from the chancellor." I knew that Roger had strong views about many things and disagreement with some of the things I believed in and discussed in my remarks to the faculty. And I knew that if I became the dean, Roger could become part of a no-holds-barred opposition that might lead to a serious grudge or two. Yet I wasn't quite ready for this. "Randy, I repeat, don't do it. You will be a terrible dean; it will eat you up alive. I know it and you know it."

"Roger, I simply do not understand."

"Randy, don't be coy with me. I know you too well. You are popular with students and with colleagues for good reason: you like being liked. You feed off of approval especially through friendships. You work at it and hard. Some cozy up to popularity by appeasement, sometimes by giving students what they want and not what they need. That's not you. You are a demanding teacher much appreciated by students over time. And they see you as fair, supportive, and giving, which go a long way towards approval. And there is something comparable for colleagues. You are not threatening. Think about it. As a long-time chair of our curriculum committee, you are a master of negotiation and keeping colleagues happy with illusions that they each got what they wanted. This has been your guiding principle, but it won't work as the dean. Certainly not all of the time. Hard decisions are inevitable, and so are unhappiness, bitterness, and even enemies. And your mantra since I've known you is don't make enemies. That's impossible. You will have enemies and they will make life miserable, and one of them could be me."

Roger's lecture was a lot to take in; I didn't like it. I wanted to say something, but before I could, Roger had more. "Randy, I have known many deans in my time, some here and more elsewhere. The most successful are those that come from without. Not those from in-house, except during really good times when a school prospers and everyone is happy. And those who come from without or within seldom stay long-term. Often they go elsewhere because of friendships never made or because of friendships lost. Tough decanal decisions that affect people, and they always do, have consequences like unhappiness and inevitable distance. And sometimes, ex-deans eventually move on because of difficult, or at least awkward, transition from the deanship to a mere faculty member. Deans are accustomed to the trappings of power. They control salaries and influence matters of courses, committees, and certainly promotions. And once they step down to the faculty, many find it difficult, if not painful, to bite their tongue and refrain from entering and sometimes dominating debate instead of withholding their opinion and giving a new dean some space. Power breeds ego, and the power that accompanies leadership can be intoxicating. Some deans have described the transition as a step up to the faculty. But that's nonsense. Less and less, former deans simply return to the faculty and continue their career as teachers and scholars. Instead, they remain in the business of higher education administration. Sometimes as provosts, chancellors, or other high-up administrators. Or sometimes with foundations connected to higher education and important issues of policy. And this redirection usually sticks. At center are the luster and excitement of leadership and power and the challenge of things new. Perhaps also are the boredom of past class preparation and the challenge and excitement of administrative multi-tasking of daily crises. Perhaps often it reflects the fatigue of teaching and the originality demanded by cutting edge scholarship. Indeed, educators find their long-term career paths in different ways. So Randy, I ask you: who are you? I think I know, I really know. You are a born teacher who excels at teaching and inspiration. And you achieve your goals because you are effective and highly respected and almost always liked. You thrive on that. Do you want something else that may lead you elsewhere perhaps never to return? I think not. You are a great teacher, and I am confident you will be a failure as the dean." And with that Roger simply stood-up to his full marine like six feet four inches, did an abrupt about-face, and exited my office.

I continued to sit at my round conference table quietly, peacefully, but not at peace. Within moments I felt agitation, but specifics escaped me. Roger's message was clear, but was it a smoke screen for things ulterior? He distrusted clinical education and found students irrelevant to committees and law school governance. And I did not. Yet he was my mentor, my friend, my favorite colleague. He simply would not deploy a smoke screen, even one founded on truths, to remove me and my potential threat to an agenda he embraced. He would simply say it directly, straight-away, and without apology. But yet I felt kicked in the stomach, not breathless, but still accompanied by the pain of a blow that empties the gut of all air. I simply could not escape the obvious, what Roger actually said. Am I really that vain? Am I really that other driven? Approval. Is that really my quest and the center of my being as a teacher? Don't make enemies. Likeability! Better yet, negotiated solutions that yield harmony. What's so terrible about that? Paralysis, perhaps. Or bad decisions that lead nowhere or make things worse; decisions that rupture friendships and reputation; decisions that turn life on end and ultimately departure for a life elsewhere, unknown, uncertain, and unsecure for both me and Berke. I could not concentrate on anything further, and so I left my office for home, changed my clothes, and went for a run to find clarity and exhaustion, but found neither.

After supper, Berke took me aside. "Randy, you look awful. What's wrong? Please talk to me, you said you would."

"Berke, decision time has arrived, because I must move out and on from consideration if I am consumed by ambivalence about accepting an offer. To save face and goodwill, I must withdraw before an offer to me becomes public or rumored. And I think an offer is likely any day. You got me thinking weeks ago, and today Roger pushed me to my limits in telling me I would be a lousy dean. Yes, I am more than troubled, and I feel as if I am headed for disaster if I stay the course. But I can't quite let go. I need reason I can embrace and feel. I need to work it through alone."

"Randy, I understand. I expected this." And with that, I retreated to my study in further pursuit and hope for clarity.

But clarity did not appear while awake or in fitful sleep through the night. I imagined every scenario possible about what life would be like. What if? What if? With my training at work, another what if, and then another, and then another. I also imagined unrecovered loss of precious time with my two children. What regrets, both mine and theirs? And what about Berke and unfulfilled promise? Inevitably, thoughts drifted back to ME. ME. What if I was a failure as dean and had to move on to life unknown? But throughout, everything was punctuated with, in and out, glimpses of life without teaching, life without students, life without the excitement of new and exciting classes and friendships reborn every autumn. A life I knew and had loved. But still no clarity. Finally morning, daylight, unease, and still decision time. I arose and left for school before others had awakened. I had decided.

Actually I had decided to decide. Indecision had forced the issue in my mind. Decision by default to remain doing what I had done seemed far better than becoming a dean by default. I called the chancellor's office, asked for an appointment that day, and said it was important. I didn't have to wait long. Dan Thomas's secretary called me back immediately with an appointment at noon. Once again, I arrived early, and once again, I was greeted by Dan and Martin Fainsod. Without niceties or preamble, I got right to the point. "Dan and Martin, I am withdrawing from consideration as dean. And I wanted Dan to know immediately, hopefully before he made his selection."

Dan immediately interrupted. "But why? Martin just returned, and I was ready to make a selection after reviewing it with him. We began the process with you as front runner, and you have been front runner throughout. I am stunned and disappointed."

"Dan, it just didn't feel right for many reasons. Mainly, I became a candidate because it seemed to be the next step in academia. But I am not sure that's what I need or where I want to be. And I did not wish to begin something as important as this uncertain, half-hearted, and uncommitted. That's not fair to you, the school, or my colleagues. I only wish I had realized this from the outset."

Dan and Martin looked at each other in dismay, and then Dan said: "Then I guess it would be pointless to try to persuade you otherwise." They both stood up to signal dismissal, and I left to teach a class and then home. Throughout the day I replayed the meeting in my mind. I should not have been surprised by their reaction. Both Dan and Martin had begun their academic careers as teachers and scholars, and they were good ones. But their last twenty years had been in administration, which they were also good at. They were disappointed, perhaps more than that. At that moment I wished I had said NO and never become a candidate.

Berke arrived home late in the day and immediately found me in my study sitting in an easy chair with a blank stare, a book before me, not reading, and transfixed by nothingness. "Randy, are you OK?"

"Yes, I guess so. I am no longer a candidate. We are back to the life we have had."

"Randy, did you achieve clarity? Do you feel any better?"

"No and not really."

And all Berke said in reply was: "I think you will and will."

———————

As I relate these events many years later, I ask the same questions. Clarity — it never arrived as clarity, but over time it sort of crept up on me as gradual recognition. I had the best of times with my two children, quality time and lots of it. Three-hour summer lunch breaks for an easy trip to the zoo, track and cross-country meets, student plays and musicals, coaching hockey, and more. Our daughter died at age fifty-three, and without this quality time, wonderful memories would have been replaced by consumptive guilt. As for Berke? She emerged as a true star impacting the lives of many kindergarteners and first graders who as adults remember her as a great teacher. But this was the easy part of self-recognition and enough to justify my decision.

Apart from Berke, daughter, and son, did I make the right choice? What if this opportunity had arisen ten years later or should I have pursued a deanship at a later time? In my day, most people held one job and did so for life, unlike today. We were children born of the depression when parents struggled because jobs were non-existent, and those that did arise were precious keepers. That mentality became part of the psyche of my generation. A tenured appointment seemed like gold, never to be abandoned. But that doesn't explain my decision because the tenured appointment wouldn't have evaporated upon becoming the dean of the Eliot School of Law. Still, changing career direction involved, as it often does, risk taking with high reward if successful. But are these high rewards better or worth the risk when one is essentially happy as is? At the time, I knew that I was happy and treasured the professional life I had. I did fear burn-out, and I did yearn to repeat the mountain I had climbed and relive the excitement and exhilaration of new conquests. I couldn't fabricate the mountain, but I was able to refresh my work as a scholar with new and different projects. That was the easy part. But what of my teaching? Aren't there limits to mastering pedagogy and subject matter? Over time I learned otherwise. The learning curve for committed teachers is a constant, and the direction is always up, especially for classes taught with interactive discussion. Something more is always there waiting to be discovered and perfected. How people think, how they comprehend, and how they solve problems. How people react and how to detect their reactions. And if one listens to students carefully enough, a teacher may discover elements of new ideas, true originality, that may spark ground-breaking and creative scholarship or methodologies for teaching complicated concepts or skill-sets. Because of this, every ten years, I firmly believed that I had become a better teacher and scholar than the decade before.

Do I ever think of what might have been? Yes, I do. But mostly this occurs when I witness a dean stumble in ways that I would not and then convince myself that I would have been good at it because somehow the admonition of Roger Davis—that I am approval driven and would make a lousy dean—sticks in my craw. Sometimes I speculate further and wonder what if? What if? What if? And when I do, I remind myself of the thousands of bright and inspiring minds and friendships I would never have known. Is this clarity? I don't know; nevertheless it is always enough.

CHAPTER 6

THE REUNION

E. Randall Mann

The instructions were clear. The address was 29 Willow Road, a winding two lane suburban thoroughfare that featured large homes among hills and valleys. Willow Road was well known and easy to find, but 29 was not. The number stood atop a discolored wooden mailbox that was partially hidden by overgrown bushes. It signaled an address that was not meant to be found. Several passes were made before we knew we had arrived.

Yet still it seemed to be the wrong place. We turned right and entered something strange and unexpected. We proceeded almost a half mile through a forest of tall trees that blocked out all evidence of a setting sun. And there it was—a modest home to our right and a small road that led up a hill revealing two large buildings that resembled castles. But there was also evidence of a golf course that meandered through the valley and up the hill. On my left was the largest green I had ever seen surrounded by traps with sand that was pure white. The fairways were in immaculate condition with freshly cut grass. But which golf course could this be? I could not recall any at this location or nearby. Nothing seemed to make sense. Except to my wife Berke. "Randy, it's quite simple. On the right must be the caretaker's home, and the biggest castle up there is his. I am sure! Just follow the yellow brick road." I sat there unsure. Why had we come, and what was to come?

I had been teaching at the Eliot University School of Law for twenty-eight years, and we were about to attend a twenty-fifth reunion with the class that had arrived with me. They had been a very special class; in a sense, we had grown up together. They became professionals, while I learned to know what it really meant to teach and become a teacher. The class that began was small, eighty students divided into two sections, and I taught the first year course on property to both sections. By today's standards, it was a small entering class, and it became even smaller by graduation, under sixty students mainly because of natural and forced attrition. I knew them each by name and hoped to recognize all by sight despite their twenty-five year journey from young adulthood to mid-life.

The original eighty were not diverse, certainly not by today's metrics. Although many attended college elsewhere, nearly all were born and raised locally. There were three women, all White. Two of the male students were Negroes, the term of respect that was to transition to Black and then African-American. Two were Asian, one of Japanese ancestry and the other of Chinese. And the rest of the class consisted of White males. Some had spent several years in the Army, including one student who had fought in the Battle of the Bulge as an eighteen year old. Two had been in the Air Force, including one who was on active duty monthly flying throughout North America and beyond, while the other was moonlighting as a commercial pilot for a major airline on weekends. Although the class included Republicans and Democrats, both groups were much more alike than not. They were from middle class and above backgrounds, intact families, educated parents or parents who valued education, centrists on most issues, and not inclined to make waves as teenagers or college students. They wanted success but were not motivated to change the world. They were younger than me, yet products of the same generation. Little difference between teacher and student existed except for the J.D., several years of practice, and a teaspoonful of life experience.

They were also very bright. By today's admission requirements, most would have been borderline admits at best. Nonetheless, they would have stood out as very smart in any group then and now. They loved to talk and debate. And they pushed me in class and beyond with unexpected questions and responses that were frightening for a teacher merely two weeks ahead of them in terms of the casebook and assignments. Some were screw-ups and some flirted with failure, but most worked hard. Yet none had much fun with law school. They despised some teachers but respected others, not unlike students at other law schools. Although I could not be sure, I hoped I was remembered as respected. I suppose that was why I had chosen to attend and commandeered Berke for moral support. With twenty-five years in between, maybe tonight I would discover that I had made it as a teacher with them.

Out of the entire group, I saw several on occasion in the intervening twenty-five years. Some had settled elsewhere in the Midwest or on both coasts and had become remote geographically. And all had settled into busy lives professionally and at home that left little time for non-working lunches with former teachers or alumni events with boring speeches and solicitations perceived to be at the core. This reunion was also a first. The school did not have one for graduates of five, ten, and fifteen years, and this class could not manage much interest in a twentieth. But they did for their twenty-fifth. Sixty people had registered for the dinner, forty were graduates, and the rest were spouses or partners. This was an exceptional turnout in light of merely fifty survivors among them.

The attraction could have been a need to reunite, something that often accompanies age, maturity, and satisfaction with one's place in life. But it was also a free dinner at a palatial estate. Even more, there was intrigue. Our host, presumably a classmate, was unknown. No one could determine his identity. Not even our dean or Alumni and Development at the University. The offer to host the reunion came through an intermediary, a lawyer, who was not a classmate. This lawyer could and did disclose that our host was a member of the class but he was ordered not to reveal this classmate's identity. The University and several classmates tried to solve the mystery. Real estate records for 29 Willow Road listed ownership by a trust with an impenetrable listing of beneficiaries. All real estate taxes were paid by this trust, but so far as one could tell, no one was currently residing at this home. Drive by visits to the address revealed nothing. Yet the invitation seemed to be real, including the invitation list provided by the secret host.

Everything seemed to be legitimate and enticing. The host made all arrangements for the evening with an invitation that described the entertainment — a performance by a renowned jazz quartet — and a dinner menu rich with choices and delicacies and a wine list that included bottles worth a thousand dollars and up. At first, the events staff from Alumni and Development didn't know what to do. Was this for real? If it wasn't, this reunion would be a disaster. And with it, all benefits to a twenty-fifth reunion — including generous gifts — would be lost, especially for a class that hadn't been interested in reunions. But the reunion committee for the class was caught up in the venue, the menu, and the mystery. They simply wanted to know who, and probably why as well. As did I.

And so Berke and I proceeded up the yellow brick road with excitement and, at least for me, a measure of trepidation. When we arrived atop the hill, the two buildings seemed even larger than from down below. One was apparently the principal home. But we couldn't immediately find the "front entrance." There appeared to be a main entrance and elaborate doorway off the veranda that ran the full length of the building overlooking the valley below. Yet the door was closed and deserted. There was, however, an entrance on the side of this building and as we got closer we saw that valet parking was already underway, and it was there that we left our car and entered a world beyond expectation. We emerged into a hallway that led to a great room with a ceiling that rose high above anything I had ever seen in a private home. We were among the first to arrive, and were immediately greeted by servers prepared to wait on every whim and wish of guests. They were all male and dressed in business attire, specifically charcoal grey or navy suits. One asked for our names, scanned the guest list and placed a check-mark besides our names. But there were no name tags as there always were at university events. I inquired and was told that was simply the way our host wanted it. Berke was immediately pleased. She intensely disliked them, mainly because alumni ordinarily cared little about faculty wives, their names, and anything meaningful about them. She smiled and said: "Randy, this is my kind of evening, so let's move on down the road!" My eyes wandered the hallway and great room searching for familiar faces, especially the mystery host. I asked about his whereabouts, then and thereafter, and was informed that our host would appear later that evening.

We entered the great room that was filled with antique furniture, art objects, and paintings that occupied its enormous walls. In one corner was a grand piano with Ben Wilson, the best jazz pianist in town, at the keyboard. But there was no one present to listen. The room was without people and seemed like a museum after hours. But for the music, there was a stony sense of silence and cold, an environment with human depictions but not humanity. We were told that two separate tours of the premises would be announced and conducted for guests that were interested, but meanwhile, we should proceed out to the patio where other guests had gathered. And so we were led through a sitting room to open doors that revealed an enormous patio large enough to comfortably seat at least several hundred people. It was a beautiful autumn evening in the low seventies with a very light breeze. The immediate view of the valley below, the setting sun, and the golf course bathed in several shades of green was spectacular, and also something that had gone unobserved from below. There was a small lake that was home to four white swans. At first I thought they were unreal, but flap their wings and swim they did. We stood there for a moment, silent and mesmerized by the sheer beauty of the moment. But the sound of voices on the patio reminded me that others were here with familiar faces hopefully in accompaniment.

Berke followed as we turned a corner to find three couples in animated conversation. As we approached them, I immediately was seized with unease. I recognized no one. Not one. Some of the voices seemed familiar but not the faces or the bodies that accompanied them. Three men turned toward us and said not quite in unison: "Professor Mann." They immediately introduced their wives but did not identify themselves. Although I was THE PROFESSOR, I was nervous and uncertain. How was I to introduce Berke without using their names?

Berke understood me and my predicament immediately, took the initiative, and attempted to save me. "Hi, I am Berke, Randy's wife." They each replied with first names only, Jerry, John, and George. This didn't ring any bells of recollection. In and out of class, I knew and referred to students by last names only. This was custom. "Mr. Smith, would you please tell us the issue in *Jones v. Jones*." In terms of clues, the conversation led nowhere with small talk about the weather and home of the host. Berke was enjoying the moment. She could see my discomfort while getting a taste of what she experienced each time she accompanied THE PROFESSOR to a school event.

I whispered: "It's time to move on."

She whispered: "No, let's stay until you discover last names." When the conversation shifted focus, I grabbed Berke's arm and moved us in the direction of others whom I might recognize.

And I did. With only three women in the class, it wasn't difficult to identify each. One was apparently by herself standing on the far side of the veranda, speaking to no one, and accepting a glass of wine from a waiter taking orders and passing out drinks. "Ms. Haley?" I asked.

She turned and smiled, apparently pleased to be recognized. "Professor Mann, so good to see you."

"Ms. Haley, after all these years, please call me Randy. And if I could recall your first name, I would do the same." She was tall, still thin, attractive, poised, and appeared at age fifty the same as she did in her twenties. "Please forgive me, this is my wife Berke."

"Very good to meet you, Berke, and to see you, Professor Mann, excuse me, Randy, and please call me JoAnne." At that moment one of the servers announced that a tour of the home and premises was about to begin. With great enthusiasm Berke immediately announced that was where she was headed along with anyone wanting to join her. I begged off, wanting to visit with JoAnne and many others before dinner.

I had not kept in touch with JoAnne or had any knowledge of what she had done since graduation from law school. I had recalled her as quiet—painfully at times—but very intelligent, even though her record put her somewhere in the middle of her class. And she remained quiet and probably would have said nothing had I not asked: "JoAnne, it's been a long time. Do you mind telling me about yourself and filling in some of the years?"

She replied: "Professor Mann—Randy—are you really interested? I never imagined you would be."

I was shaken by her question, something I did not expect. My immediate emotion was insult or incivility at the very least. I was tempted to walk away, but I was the elder and the teacher and I should know better. So I said simply "YES," almost inaudibly.

She firmly replied "why?"

"What is this JoAnne? Are we back in class with a Socratic dialogue and role reversal? A kind of student revenge?"

"If you wish to call it that. Tell me, Professor Mann," and then she paused to collect her thoughts carefully. The "Professor" reflected contempt and an unwillingness to substitute "Randy" and the measure of friendship it might imply. "Do you really care how I have done with my life or even what I have done?" She then paused, and before I could answer she continued: "Better yet, what would you have predicted? A brief career on my own or with unknown second rate lawyers? Marriage? How many kids? A subsequent revival of law practice, perhaps some piece work for other lawyers? Go back in time and tell me what you probably thought or expected to see and hear tonight!"

What could I say? Honestly, I probably never even thought about predicting a life outcome for JoAnne Haley. For some others, perhaps. But not for her. But why not? She wasn't an academic star or stand-out personality among those classmates for whom success seemed a sure thing, nor did she flirt with failure in school, and probably not in professional life either. Further, JoAnne Haley was a woman, and for her generation, good jobs and success were a steep uphill climb. Large prominent law firms had no women partners, few women associates, and seldom sought or hired women who might apply. JoAnne and many other students—men and women—simply never appeared on my radar screen for prediction. Nor did I expect to see them here tonight or really care about seeing them here tonight. I did, however, hope to see others, those who were the most talented and engaging. And that meant the men in JoAnne's class and not the few women. And so I spoke the truth: "JoAnne, sharing some kind of prediction about you would be pure fiction. I never gave your future a thought. Simple as that."

"Professor Mann, then let me fill you in on my last twenty-five years. But before I do, I must tell you what it was like to apply to law school, to attend law school, and to be one of your students. I was a very good student at my small liberal arts college for women in Pennsylvania; in fact, I graduated second in my class. I always wanted to be a lawyer. I did not have to confront the draft, so I thought I would apply immediately and hope for both admission and a healthy scholarship, because in my family, there had been no money for college without the full scholarship I received and would be none for law school either. You may recall that many law schools required interviews, and most did among the schools I applied to, but Eliot University School of Law did not. Those that did bombarded me with questions. 'Why did I apply? What did I intend to do with my education. Work? For how long, a few years? We are very careful with our admits because of limitations on enrollment. Spaces must go to those who deserve them and will do the most with the opportunity. Experience tells us this seldom includes women. And one other thing. We do not waste scholarships on women.' But you see, Professor Mann, Eliot was different. No interview and no discouraging questions or statements. And so I applied and was rewarded with admission and a full scholarship. I was very excited and hopeful about Eliot and my legal education and career that lay just ahead.

"It didn't take long, however, for my optimism to deflate. At orientation, I noticed only three women and almost thirty times as many men. But the Dean also sounded an alarm when he announced that only the top third at the end of the first year would retain their scholarships. Supposedly, this fact appeared in the school's published bulletin. If it did, I never saw it. I immediately calculated my chances. Top third, I had always done that easily. But I had competed only with women. Yet I could do it, somehow I would. But I didn't, and you were part of the reason. You gave me the lowest grade I have ever received, and it was a grade I never expected and thought unfair. It was a C+ and I never before had received anything less than an A-. It was by far my lowest grade in law school. And without a scholarship, I was certain my career in law had ended."

I remained silent. What could I say? Grading was anonymous. I had no recollection of her paper or having conferred with her about it after she received her grade. C+ was not a bad grade; it was around the middle of the class and paralleled her classroom performance. Yet I did feel compelled to say something. I still wanted to be cordial. "JoAnne, why didn't you come see me about any of this, especially your exam preparation or ultimately your concern with the result and losing your scholarship? I might have been able to help."

"Professor Mann, that's after the fact revisionism and unmitigated bullshit! I was never on your radar screen, so I could never put you on mine. In class, you were Professor Kingsfield incarnate, unequaled and untouchable. Despite your youth, you were better at Kingsfield than John Houseman himself. Your Socratic method tortured us with confrontation and uncertainty and made me think again and again about my choice of legal education. Always confrontation. I was not accustomed to that, not expecting that, and not wanting that as a student and a woman. But, of course, being a woman or the relevance of a woman's perspective were meaningless to you. We were invisible as sources of talent and success. Well not quite. Except for Ladies Day. One day a week, you and your colleagues would call on us in class. The only day we were acknowledged for anything. The dialogue was brief, the questions were softballs, and the atmosphere reeked of condescension. The implication was clear: our analyses, ideas, and opinions were worthless and warranted little recognition. Why waste your time and brilliant mind? More important, why should we waste our time and come to you for anything, even to save us from drowning?" JoAnne's voice was now edgy and shrill. Her anger had surfaced and boiled over.

And I made things even worse when I replied: "But I did have office hours. Figuratively my door was always open. I wasn't like that. I could have helped and would have, which is something I have done again and again for students. So much could have been averted and overcome."

"Professor, once again bullshit! You still don't get it. I was a woman, and your buddies were men. Despite your Houseman classroom demeanor, you were proud of your reputation as the students' PAL. You played softball, tennis, golf, and basketball regularly with male students and even joined them on canoe trips, but this was before Title Nine and a critical mass of women law students. We weren't ever asked to join you. Professor Mann, did you know that I was a college basketball player who could beat your ass at one-on-one? Yes, who would have thought … ? Not you. The men had access to you—special access. But women did not have that access. We were never offered it or given an alternative. Women were demeaned and diminished institutionally, and you were a central figure!"

I was stunned. I thought of saying something by way of a reply, but thought better of it and remained silent.

"Professor Mann, now that was law school; a miserable experience that left me in debt for many years. Well I am no longer asking you to recall what you might have predicted for me, I ask you now to guess what I have done or accomplished."

I thought for a moment and then replied: "I won't step into that trap. I assume you wouldn't be here if you hadn't done well, just the same as other classmates here tonight. That's usually the way it is at reunions. I'll be damned if I will speculate and invite another 'bullshit' from you. But you tell me, exactly why are you here tonight?"

"Professor Mann, I am here tonight for three reasons, first, out of curiosity to see who attended and what they had done with their lives. Second, I am here to discover the identity of our mystery host. And last, I wanted to confront you and other faculty members to at least let you know how great you were not and the disregard and pain you inflicted for three years.

"But because you won't play the game with me, I will give you some details about the last twenty-five years. I graduated middle of the class, as you know well, with huge debts because of a failed scholarship, and no job or immediate prospects. So I left town as fast as I could and returned to my hometown of Pittsburgh and moved in with my parents. I applied to large firms with no luck, scrounged for jobs with small firms and solo practitioners, and even knocked on doors. Finally, an elderly lawyer named Clarence Savin, with his own office and an outstanding reputation as a litigator, agreed to meet me. His need was immediate because of a big case; he hired me, and my career was launched. That was the best thing that ever happened to me. Clarence was a real teacher, the best I ever had, unlike you and your colleagues. He taught me everything about analysis, persuasion, and judgment. He trusted me, counseled me, and restored faith in myself that had been brutalized in law school. And we did well together winning trials and appeals, and along the way, humbled the biggest and best firms in town. Six years later, one of them made me an offer with a partnership and money I could not refuse. Clarence was ready to retire, and I left with his blessing. My reputation blossomed even further with this firm, including important high profile cases. I was known as a lawyer who would out-work and out-prepare anyone no matter what. And I made lots of money, more than I could ever imagine or need.

"But after ten years, I was burned out, and wanted something different. So I applied to the Justice Department in D.C. and was hired immediately. Eventually, I focused on ethical issues that had across the board implications. My reputation ascended within the Department, in government nationally, locally, and even internationally, and within business. And I was happy and content with government service indefinitely. But then a friend urged me to apply my skill and knowledge set differently and urged me to create my own company to consult with governments, practicing lawyers, and businesses on ethical issues. So I took a chance and went out on my own. That was four years ago. I now employ thirty people, mostly lawyers, and I am on the hot list for representation, workshops, counsel, and solutions nationally and internationally. Professor Mann, that's it in a nutshell. Now, what do you think about that?" But JoAnne didn't wait for any reply. She turned and walked away. She may have left the reunion because I did not see her the rest of the evening. I am not sure.

But I was certain my evening was ruined. I was stunned, not by JoAnne's success story but by her attack and perception of me. Some people always look outward for answers to things unpleasant, but my inclination, compounded by my guilt-ridden upbringing, is to look inward for answers and solutions. I wondered was JoAnne spot on, is that the person I was or am? I think I know the ME of today, who I really am and how I am regarded by others, especially students. But what of my past? Who was I? During childhood? Some might say impossible to really know. But what of teenage? Adulthood should be easier. People at this reunion began law school and were students of mine in my early thirties. Shouldn't I have clarity? Was I really Kingsfield and more? I do recall my insecurities as a young teacher with no training or previous experience. And I do recall a conscious and careful embrace of formality, serious purpose, and focused dialogue with individual students for prolonged periods of time. A dialogue in which the heavy lifting would ultimately be achieved by students with teacher direction. I do remember the terror of being called upon in law school and being subjected to earlier versions of me. But I also recall the joy of reaching the desired goal, and I thought my students did as well. Some of my colleagues could be openly abusive. "That's the dumbest thing I have ever heard." And some would excuse a student from the classroom who was unprepared even though the student's unpreparedness reflected fear and not inadequate study. But that was never me. Demanding questions—original and follow-up—and high expectations as to quality, sophistication, and resourcefulness. Yes. But never abusive or demeaning language. Yet these are my recollections, not JoAnne's. Are hers skewed? A reflection of personal background and the prism that embodies her life experience? Perhaps I should turn that around. How others perceive me, especially in the classroom; the real test is not through my prism but how others experience me. Is polite language a guaranty of civility? Just one slip can blow open a reputation. It's not just the student under fire's perception; it's the reaction of the entire class. The chilling effect of the hot seat occupied by a single student may reach an entire class and thereafter descend from class to class. Worst of all, did I really demean and diminish women students? Oblivious and ignore? Perhaps. But demean and diminish? Beyond the classroom, what could I have done differently? Embrace, not ignore, women as well as invisible classmates, those who fell beyond the anointed top quarter. I was dumbfounded. Reality and truth were beyond reach.

I was confident that no one overheard our conversation or even witnessed her hostility from afar. That made no difference. I was injured, deflated, and ready to depart with no hope of receiving remembrance, respect, accolades, and the warm embrace of reuniting. This is why I attended. I searched for Berke but could not find her. So I found a corner and stood there sulking and hoping no one would discover me. But the bar was nearby. After two vodkas straight-up, I was prepared for the rest of the evening. Within minutes, four men appeared at the bar. I immediately recognized the voices and the faces, but not the bodies that had widened considerably. And immediately I was able to assign last and first names to all four. I had known each very well. They were shining stars in my property class, on their exams, and in and out of the classroom. They were very bright, personable, and lots of fun. They constituted almost the entire editorial board of the Law Review, the best of the best. I could almost close my eyes, locate their classroom seats, and hear their voices and responses. They were a breath of fresh air then, and even more important this night.

I could hear myself calling on Mr. Harris. Mr. Gordon. Mr. Brown. Mr. Hall. None would cringe or even hide. And most of the time I would find a smile illuminating their faces, especially when they understood and could anticipate both my direction and misdirection. They were the "go-to" people every teacher needed to overcome a dead-end discussion. Even more, their expressive faces telegraphed what they were thinking—consternation, confusion, dismay, ah ha moments, and disagreement—and probably what others were as well. They were exceptional. Each gave me model exam papers that I used for years in teaching subsequent generations of students. With this group, I could ask, "what have you been doing the past twenty-five years" and know with confidence that I would hear good things and wouldn't be shot down in the process. I greeted them and they responded enthusiastically and warmly as my funk dissipated. They encircled me as one by one we exchanged news of family and health. Health was good, but marriage and the families that went with them were multiple. Soon the single conversation among us broke up and dissolved into twos and threes.

I then turned to Mike Brown, who thus far had been silent, and said, "Mike I know the answer to what you have been doing these past twenty-five years, all I have had to do was follow the decisions of the United States Supreme Court." Mike was indeed well known within the field of property. He lived in Southern California and represented wealthy real estate developers with respect to litigation lost by other lawyers in trial court. In each instance, there was at stake both money and legal principle, and so an appeal was taken to a higher court. And Mike was the very best appellate lawyer, so good that lawyers in California consistently voted him among the top five of all lawyers within the state. His legal specialty was eminent domain, and he made law several times before the Supreme Court that changed the landscape of property rights. He had also made a name for himself as a scholar with upwards of fifty important law review articles. Mike was also a popular lecturer at law schools and conferences; indeed, he was on everyone's "A list." But as I awaited his reply, it suddenly dawned on me that my recollections reflected information that may have been stale. I hadn't read or heard anything involving Mike Brown in the last few years.

Before responding, Mike paused for a long time just as he did as a student. Finally, he said: "Randy, my life has changed dramatically; I have given up law for something else." And then there was an even longer pause. Expecting further response, I waited. "Randy, you may recall, that as a student I was older, married, and had three children. You may not have known, however, that I was a member of the Church of Jesus Christ of Latter-day Saints. I was raised in Salt Lake City, attended Brigham Young University, did my missionary work in West Africa, and then came to Eliot Law School. Following graduation, we settled in Los Angeles, and I did very well while achieving most every goal I had." And then another long pause followed by: "My life had been good. My children were out of school, married, and well established. But my wife became ill. Breast cancer, then surgery, then chemo, then remission, then recurrence, then more treatment, and finally death. And I was devastated. But I wasn't defeated, because of my faith and my Church. You may not know, but I have returned home after having been called back. I am now the provost of Brigham Young University. Randy, we have lots to discuss, but a different occasion is called for, something much more private."

"Mike, I am so sorry. I didn't know, I simply didn't realize…" I paused without completing the sentence or the thought.

But Mike picked up immediately. "Randy, no need to be sorry. The struggle and decline of Judy was long and courageous. And it was a difficult and painful time for her and me, but it brought us even closer together. I was devastated, but I have survived and am beginning to witness sunshine each day. No one goes through life unscathed, but I have had a good one and without regret. I love academia. I think that is where I was really meant to be. Why all the law review articles and teaching gigs if it wasn't preparation for my next career? And Randy, I will soon be remarried to a wonderful person whom I want you to meet. In fact she is a law professor at Brigham Young. I think you will like her. As a teacher, she sort of reminds me of you, persistent and unyielding. But let's save this for next time. To be continued, I hope, and soon."

I nodded and hugged him as if to say "of course." And then Mike turned and left to reunite with other classmates. I paused, watched him walk away, and then looked for other familiar faces.

Off to the side and sitting by a corner of the bar was someone recognizable and familiar. He was by himself, which surprised me. I expected him to be leading the pack of Harris, Gordon, Brown, and Hall as he did in law school. But he wasn't. He was alone and seemed uncomfortable. This wasn't the Sam Prosecco I had known. Sam was destined for success, really assured of success. He was very bright, articulate, handsome, and confident almost to the point of arrogance. He was also opinionated, yet he could argue any point from any direction, including defending the indefensible. He was both a lightning rod for disagreement and a magnet for friendship. He was flat-out good at everything he did, including athletics. People gravitated to him. Almost everyone predicted greatness, including his faculty at the Eliot School of Law. Managing partner of a major firm he founded, perhaps. CEO of a Fortune 500 company, perhaps. U.S. Senator, perhaps. University President, probably not. Make millions, to be sure! Sam was born to money and a family history of generosity in deed and spirit. And others always expected more of the same from Sam.

I began to walk towards Sam and as I got closer I observed some dramatic changes in his appearance. His blond hair had thinned and greyed and his face had become lined and full. His figure was no longer trim and his business suit looked worn and rumpled. Most of all, his expression was grim, unlike the warm and friendly smile I had known twenty-five years earlier. As I approached him, he turned his head and saw me. His face frozen, still grim.

"Sam, it's good to see you."

He replied simply "hello" without more.

"Sam, would you prefer that I leave you alone?"

"Professor Mann, that's up to you."

"What's wrong?" I said. But before he replied, I added: "Let's go over and join your buddies from law school."

"Not yet, I'm not quite ready to see them. I am gathering my strength and courage."

Again, I said: "Sam, what's wrong?"

Sam remained seated, while I stood looking down directly. The silence seemed forever, yet there was no indication he wanted me to leave. As he began to speak, he did not rise or look up at me; instead, Sam looked straight ahead, unwilling to offer eye contact. Although as a student he was the first to break tradition and call me Randy, he now addressed me with formality only. "I suppose, Professor, you never expected this incarnation of Sam Prosecco twenty-five years later. Well, neither did I. I was destined for success however one might measure it. I was raised and groomed for it. I knew it was my destiny and probably so did you and my classmates. I had it all and wanted more. Yet it did not happen; perhaps, never meant to be. What happened? Plain and simple, I failed at about everything. As you may recall, upon graduation I began my professional life with the Justice Department, Civil Rights Division, in D.C., and for a year, I helped oversee registration of voters in Mississippi and Alabama. But two years later, my family insisted I return to carry on with the family business, Mid-Western Hardware Stores. My father was set to retire, and I was his anointed successor. And for me, this looked good. It seemed like the perfect ticket to everything. But I never paid my dues or learned the business; I took everything for granted as I played at being a CEO. I made mistake after mistake as to financial and personnel issues. I fucked up big time; I was a complete failure." His speech cadence had been lightning fast, almost as if had he not blurted it out, he might never say it. But then there was another pause as he seemed to collect himself but not his thoughts. When he resumed, his speech was very deliberate and barely audible. A pause and deep breath laced the end of every sentence. It was painful to listen and to watch, yet I had invited his sharing. Sam then continued: "Ten years later, we liquidated the business, but I blew my share of the proceeds within the next five. By this time I had been married and divorced twice with one child to support from each. My third marriage also failed; thank goodness, no more children to support. The fact is I couldn't hold a job. I was broke. I still am. My children won't even see me or speak to me. Worst of all, my health is failing. I look like shit; you don't have to tell me. My body has really broken down. I am diabetic and my eye sight is diminished. My kidneys are in bad shape and probably my heart as well. That's the story, Professor Mann."

"Sam, then why did you attend your reunion? I am still glad to see you, but why are you putting yourself in the spotlight of failed promise?"

"Professor Mann, I honestly don't know. I suppose I was curious about others, perhaps hoping there were classmates who had failed at something or for whom success was not a constant. Perhaps I simply wanted to say goodbye." And then another pause, but this time I did not anticipate more.

"Sam, do you mind if we go over there together? I know your buddies will be happy to see you; they have already asked about you."

"Professor, please don't lie. They will be shocked to see me. Never happy to see me, except maybe happy they aren't me. Besides, I am not able to walk over there alone; I need my inspiration, Tammy. She is my fourth wife, a real 'keeper.' I could not exist without her. Thanks anyway." Sam then turned his head, looked to the floor, and closed his eyes. "Goodbye, Professor." And that was all. I had been excused.

I backed away. At that moment, Berke came running over enthusiastic and excited as only she could be. "Randy, I have just been through a museum and more. Come with me. I have permission to show you some of what I have just seen." But I was slow to respond. Berke looked at me and immediately understood something upsetting had happened. "OK, what happened? This was supposed to be a good time, that's why I came, and that's what I'm having."

"Berke, it's simply not the time I expected or hoped for; it's a long story that I will relate later." Berke was good with that, so off we went to explore in the time that remained before we were called to supper. The highlights included an exceptional collection of twentieth century paintings, a study with multiple telephones and television sets, a collection of well-known books on history and politics (yet none involving law), a wine cellar with at least a few thousand bottles, a guest washroom with hidden handles to activate the toilet and the faucets, and a second building that housed a racket ball court, swimming pool, a room with weights and aerobic equipment, and a locker room with all the amenities. After this, I was even more curious as to the identity of the owner and host for the evening. If I had had to guess before we arrived, it would have been Sam Prosecco. I dared not guess again.

As we reentered the main building, guests were assembling for dinner in a huge dining room that seated everyone. There was no assigned seating. Classmates had been talking with best friends and were searching for table space that enabled them to carry-on with their mini-reunions. We were late comers and had to find two places wherever available. A pattern had already been established, classmates with classmates and faculty with faculty. Although there were merely four former teachers present along with their wives, this was a good turnout. They all found seating at the corner of an end table. They reserved two places for us, something Berke and I had wished to avoid. We saw colleagues all of the time, and more of the same Berke labeled as boring. She was right. I had wanted to connect with all of the students I had known and liked, but this had now become impossible. My engagement with them beforehand had been focused and limited. And after dinner, the evening would soon conclude, and everyone would go their separate way. Not enough reuniting, and I felt short-changed. I expressed this to Berke, but she did not sympathize. "Randy, that's you. You simply are unable to work a room going from person to person with some small talk for each. You have to ask questions that demand responses. Worst of all, you actually listen and then ask another question that leads to something meaningful. If you want something different, then be something different, which you will never do."

So we sat through a boring dinner with my colleagues and spouses refreshing old conversations of the past. Occasionally I attempted small talk with others across the table, but distance and acoustics made anything significant impossible. The meal, however, was outstanding. There was an array of appetizers shared family style along with choices as to entrees and wines comparable to the best restaurants. I had sea bass encrusted in salt, and Berke ordered the short ribs; they were both outstanding. Finally, three different desserts were presented along with after dinner drinks. Ben Wilson then introduced the remainder of his quartet and a Sinatra sound-alike who gave us music from our collective past. But then the music stopped, and the conversation hushed, as if the moment we had waited for was about to arrive. The identity of our host had been something discussed and debated before and during dinner.

Finally, a server, who had tended bar and also functioned as the head waiter, seemed to emerge from nowhere in the center of the room with a hand held microphone. And he was accompanied by total silence. The gentleman then cleared his throat and began: "I am here to ask questions and answer questions about this evening."

Before he could continue further, someone shouted: "I have but one, who is our host and classmate?"

The gentleman paused as silence merged into coughs, stirrings, and impatience. Finally, he replied: "The answer is simple, but I had also hoped it would be obvious. I AM YOUR HOST AND CLASSMATE!"

Again there was silence, stone cold silence in disbelief. Again someone shouted: "Who are you? What's your name?"

He replied: "But first I wish to ask: Does anyone recognize me from over twenty-five years ago?" The gentleman who had previously served us was of slight build and about five feet, ten inches tall. He had black hair, was clearly of Asian heritage, and he spoke without any accent. The class had two Asian students and, as I recalled, both had graduated, although many other classmates had not. Our host was the only Asian present. I remembered the name of the other student, but he had not made the trip from Honolulu where he had lived except for his time in law school.

Frustrated, I leaned over and whispered to Berke: "I have no idea who he is." Nor did anyone else. Our host waited for some response, but there were only murmurs without answers.

Finally, he said: "I am not surprised. My name is Ricky Goo, now does that mean anything to you?" I had always prided myself on mastering and remembering the names of my students because, at the very least, it facilitated effective orchestration of class discussion. Yet Ricky Goo meant nothing to me. I couldn't believe it had been fully erased for me and apparently everyone else that was present, assuming we had held onto the name at all years ago. Again there was collective discomfort because of prolonged silence.

Finally, Ricky Goo continued. "Although disappointed, I am not surprised. In short, here is my story. My parents made their way from China during World War II to Taiwan where I was born as the war ended. When I was ten, my parents came to the United States and settled in Dallas, Texas. I never spoke English until I began school in this country. I attended San Francisco State for college with a full scholarship. Following graduation, I worked for two years as a translator and then came to Eliot School of Law because a job awaited me with Professor Jolson who needed help in translating Chinese statutes. Unfortunately, most of you did not know him, because he died during our first year of school. He had become my mentor, and then he was gone. And I was lost.

"No one here knew me or cared. I always sat in the last row in one corner or another always frightened and with nothing to say. I sat with my head lowered and probably walked the halls the same. I spoke with an accent and probably choked on every uttered word. At first, teachers called on me but quickly gave up. Their impatience and yours were striking. But soon I was safe. I became an anonymous occupant of a seat in every class. Within the law school and university community, I was a nonentity. I ate by myself and lived by myself. I had no support and little confidence. I wore thick glasses. Now, do any of you remember? MISTER MAGOO. Do you recall that name, the one you pinned on me? Yet I stayed with it and graduated. All things considered, I did well academically, or at least better than half of you.

"After graduation I returned to San Francisco where I could surround myself with others who looked and spoke like me. I applied to the California Bar but was denied admission because I was not a U.S. citizen. What seemed like the end, however, was just the beginning. I soon found my future: Shoes. Basketball, tennis, sandals and the like. The demand nationally and internationally for basketball shoes had exploded. I contacted friends of my parents who were still living in Taiwan, and a business venture, my first, was born. We made shoes for major companies that branded their products with the names of big time players in the N.B.A. And we made them better and cheaper. Ten years out of law school I had amassed a fortune. And that was only the beginning. Today, I own most of the commercial planes you fly. I own them and lease them, yes, I am the lessor. I also own real estate and developments throughout the world. How many of you regularly shop at the Gardens Mall here in town? That's me, along with the high rise office building across the street. That's my story, one you would not have imagined and still may not comprehend or believe. Stay as long as you wish this evening." No one left, at least not at that moment, except for two of my colleagues who had already gotten up and were in the process of departing. Throughout Ricky Goo's coming out and revelations, I had seen them repeatedly shaking their heads in disbelief, disapproval, and even dismissal.

Ricky Goo then turned as if to immediately leave the room, but he stopped when someone asked aloud: "Is this your home?"

He responded: "Yes it's mine, one of five throughout the world, but I am not here very often and seldom use it."

Someone then asked: "This is more than a home; it's a showpiece like nothing else around here or perhaps anywhere. Why have it at all or continue to have it?"

Our host thought for a moment before replying. "I find it comfortable when I am here, more so than a Holiday Inn, and continuing to own it does not make a dent financially. Perhaps, that is not answer enough. Quite frankly, I was waiting many years for this moment, the opportunity afforded by our reunion. I wanted to impress you, even shock you. MISTER MAGOO. Would you believe it! Even someone like me has something to offer and is worth knowing. Always look around you. What is it they said to us on the first day of class: look to your right, your left, in front, and behind you; one will be gone by graduation? I would advise: look to all four, because each is worth knowing." With that Ricky Goo waved good bye, walked into the night, and departed with a limousine that had been waiting.

With that, the evening came to a screeching halt. Goodbyes were swift with no one hanging around to post mortem the evening. At least not then and there. Classmates probably did rendezvous elsewhere or the next day. Their reactions had to be considerable. I grabbed Berke's arm and hurriedly made our way to the valet parking. "What's the rush?" she said.

All I could think of was to reply "later."

Once in the car, Berke pursued my mood, which she recognized as bleak and agitated. "Randy, let's talk about it; why didn't you at least stay long enough to offer goodbyes to former students you once liked?"

After five minutes of silence, I said: "You know me better than anyone. And you already nailed me on it earlier this evening. I don't do well with 'stop-and-nods' which I always turn into a prolonged 'stop-and-chat.' And besides, I am not sure I wanted either. As we were leaving, all I was hearing from others was that this was Revenge of the Nerds—punctuated with laughter."

"Randy, what's wrong with that?" I had no reply, yet I was bothered and wanted desperately to explain my bother. But I could not, and so I remained speechless until we arrived home.

Once home, Berke would not relent: "You wanted to attend, and I accompanied you. I had a decent time, albeit with unanticipated twists and turns that made the evening strange but fascinating. What did you expect or want?"

I was reluctant to say anything, not knowing what to say. "I certainly didn't expect this. I anticipated normality, whatever that is, and probably predictability, much like my own life. But I ran into students whose names I couldn't remember, a female student who attacked me for male chauvinism, bias, condescension, unconcern, oversight, and worse, student stars whose lives unfurled as predicted, a student star whose life had crashed, and finally our host, ignored and abandoned."

"But Randy, what did you expect? That's life."

"I didn't expect being attacked individually as a teacher or as a member of the faculty."

"Randy, that's your ego; that's your arrogance getting in the way. You are not perfect, and you can't be perfect or make things perfect! Get over it! Your next twenty-five years will be more of the same."

Berke is wise, always a realist, and she made sense. Yet I could not hear or embrace it inside out. It didn't quite fit. We did not discuss this again. But I still could not let it go, then or even now. What is a teacher, and what are his responsibilities? Must a teacher make all students visible to the teacher and others within the classroom? People walk down the street, what do they see, whom do they see? The man or woman with movie star good looks? The children playful and playing? The person short or tall, white or black? Or the homeless huddled in an alley corner? Always, there are the visible and the near invisible. Is the classroom the same as the rest of life? Do we gravitate always towards those who are talented, outgoing, carefully spoken, cheerful, good-looking, articulate, and blessed with all the abilities and characteristics we deem predictors for success or even greatness? What about those who appear otherwise? Neither JoAnne Haley nor Ricky Goo satisfied these predictors as students, and, thus, remained hidden throughout from view and attention. Yet they ran rings around their classmates in the real world. But should this surprise; neither GPAs nor LSATs or classroom performance in law school are flawless predictors for even academic success. All of us have known the quiet ones who come out of the woodwork to rank their course or even class. But more important, must a teacher of law, or of any discipline, go further and endeavor to identify the invisible in need of something? What is the cost of a little time and attention?

I know how Professor Kingsfield would answer these questions, and I know how many of my colleagues at Eliot and elsewhere would respond as well. "Randy, you just don't get it. Law is a profession, and law school is a professional school. It's not grade school, high school, or even college. And it is certainly not nursery school. Judges and clients don't coddle, and neither should we. Law school is an introduction to reality, and it is not our responsibility to hold the hands of students. And they are better off if we don't. Forget about the invisible. It's their responsibility to become visible just the same as they must do with employers, clients, and partners within the real world!"

Can I really buy into that; is that kind of teacher really me? Was it, is it? Am I really Kingsfield with a conscience that inspires angst but not action? Must my radar screen include and embrace everyone? Is this possible? Have I ever tried or really wanted to? I know the answers to these questions; does it matter?

CHAPTER 7

TALES OF FEAR:
OF TEACHERS AND STUDENTS

E. Randall Mann

E very lawyer, at least those schooled during the twentieth century, recalls his first day of class, especially his first class on that first day. Central for all is fear; fear of the materials, but most of all, fear of being called upon and looking like a fool, or even worse, an idiot in the eyes of all around, not so much the professor, but most of all classmates, albeit strangers on that first day. Some say that the second most powerful remembrance is not really a remembrance of something actual, but a recurrent dream of unpreparedness in class, or even worse on a final exam. This theme of unpreparedness has also been known to morph into the courtroom for litigators and back into the classroom for law teachers. Some say the fear, and even the dreams, are worst for the conscientious and self-critical and least, perhaps even non-existent, for the boastful and arrogant. Although for law students the numbers within the latter category shift rapidly to the other after one semester of law school encounters with the Socratic method, final exams, and disappointing grades.

The basis of most student fear is the unknown. Sometimes it's the teacher's question. The "why" of it. Often, however, it's the answer. What could it possibly be; I haven't the faintest. Sometimes it's: why wasn't my answer the right answer? Or what is the right answer? Or is there ever a right answer? Where are you going with all of these questions and confusion? But underlying all of this is the public nature of this dialogue. One is asked to respond to a question, as well as a flood of follow-up questions, in front of a group of very bright people who are expected to join the discussion with agreement or disagreement often reflected with hands waiving wildly for teacher recognition. (Or these days, in front of instantaneous twitter comments from peers that appear on a classroom screen for all to see.) This is particularly disturbing to the student under fire who has not finished stating his or her position or explaining it, and is especially true for the one who has always been the smartest in the class and always on the approval end of teachers and peers.

What most students don't recognize, however, are the fears of teachers, especially the high achievers (a prerequisite of the academy) that want to be really good at what they do. Sometimes it's the fear of not receiving a promotion, most of all the one with tenure. Sometimes it's the fear of producing published scholarship that does not impress others or, much worse, falls short of one's own expectations. These kinds of fears sometime lead to paralysis that short circuits productivity or shuts it down altogether. And sometimes these fears are enough to drive one out of teaching, perhaps into administration or back to the practice of law. Yet for nearly all teachers, there is fear of the classroom, because for so many it is a total unknown. For some it's acute, for others it's mild. For some it's front burner, for others it's brushed aside. Yet it's there for all. Quite simply, young law teachers come to teaching without experience at it. It is an unknown for each. Unlike PhD candidates in other disciplines, they haven't served as teaching assistants who by the time of their first real job have withstood the fire of the classroom and odious forms of grunt work, especially grading. Some of these entry level law teachers have excelled at debate in high school, college or both. And some enter law teaching as seasoned practicing lawyers with expertise, self-assurance, and experience, especially with explanation and persuasion, both important elements of argumentation and even teaching. Yet neither may be well prepared to engineer a class discussion in which a student or group of students lead the class forward to a desired goal in which the teacher provides guidance through careful questioning (and lots of patience and persistence) and the students do the heavy lifting. And all the while, the teacher makes it seem easy, seamless, and hopefully fun, along with a dose of humor or even self-deprecation.

Fear is abundant and omnipresent in law school. Not always visible, sometimes under the radar, but always there. Tales of fear abound.

OF TEACHERS

I always pushed aside my own fears as a young teacher once I managed to overcome them. Mainly I ignored them and hoped they might never resurface. Yet I found that I could not ignore them when, after six years of teaching, I became a teacher of teachers. Tenured teachers pass judgment upon the non-tenured. They attend their classes and read their publications and they vote. But they also advise and counsel as mentors, sometimes assigned yet sometimes selected by the non-tenured teacher.

My early mentoring experiences began immediately after I was tenured at the Eliot School of Law. After six years, I was still a novice, yet entry level teachers often found it easier to discuss their concerns with someone closer in age, experience, and anxieties. Mainly, concerns were focused on tenure and what it took to achieve it. How many publications and what kind? Even what length and where to publish? Some were uncertain about the selection of topics and theses. Where would their ideas come from and could they generate originality? My replies were standard and filled with reassurance. All had written for law school journals, developed their own topics, and had their notes published. Many had practiced law for several years and had worked on problems and issues that warranted commentary. It seldom took much to transform this experience—and often expertise—into a published article, albeit one without breakthrough problem solving paradigms. Teaching seemed secondary. Most wanted to be good at it, but they never felt success depended upon it. Personal esteem perhaps, but not success. Uncertainty about the classroom—yes—but not paralyzing fear. They wanted to become a household name in their field, and publications, not teaching, were the avenue to that. So for many years, my mentoring involved a suggestion here and a nuanced change there. Seldom more. At least not until I met Christiana Nero.

I met Christiana in my thirty-fifth year of teaching at the Eliot School of Law. My earliest recollections are of her interview at the law school. Christiana had already been screened and interviewed by our Appointments Committee at the hiring convention of the American Association of Law Schools for entry level candidates. The Eliot School of Law and Eliot University were both committed to diversity, and Christiana, as a woman and African-American, qualified on two counts. She had a spectacular academic record at Central Georgia State University and Law School and after graduation had clerked with a Federal District Court Judge in Atlanta, who was one of our own alumni (and a former student of mine) and who gave her his highest and most enthusiastic recommendation. Following that, she practiced with a large prestigious law firm in Atlanta for two years. And she made the cut for intensive interviews by the entire faculty with ease and was invited to visit our school as soon as possible. Christiana was well prepared for these interviews. Specifically, Christiana had studied the background and written work of everyone who was going to interview her. And she was prepared to take charge of the interviews when the opportunity arose, typically when interviewers asked: And what questions do you have for us? Invariably, this was the interviewer's most important question, because the insight gathered from a candidate's questions made them her most important answers. So when Christiana's much anticipated opportunity to turn the tables arose, she seized it and bowled everyone over with preparation, knowledge, and persistence. Her approach was methodical — almost scripted — and careful. It also seemed confident, except when faculty members returned a question, and her voice wavered despite strong responses. She was given an offer immediately, and to our delight she accepted within two weeks' time. And so the following fall Christiana began teaching merely three years out of law school. Christiana, at less than one hundred pounds and barely five feet tall, looked even younger than her twenty-eight years. Colleagues remarked that she could even pass for a high school senior.

Christiana and I had little contact during her first month on the faculty. Occasionally, she would join some of us who liked brown bag lunches in the faculty commons. She was always cordial, listened intently to the conversation, and sometimes offered brief but meaningful comments. And then an unexpected knock on the door to my office. She asked politely whether I had a moment to speak. I invited her in, and she sat down. "Professor Mann, I need some advice."

"Christiana, we are colleagues, I much prefer Randy; in fact I require it."

"OK, Randy. I need help, maybe lots of it. I'm having a tough time teaching, a very tough time, so much so it's affecting my health." And then she paused as if to gather more courage before continuing. Yet somehow she wanted me to say something. And so I did.

"Christiana, I will do my best to help." And then there were some tears, no gut wrenching sobs, just several tears that trickled slowly down her face.

"Randy, I want to succeed at every aspect of this job; no, I must succeed. But right now, I don't know how. I have my doubts to say the least. Since day one of teaching I have been physically ill. I can't sleep, can't eat, and sometimes can barely breathe. My heart rate and blood pressure have risen to levels I've not known. And sometimes I can't think or comprehend easily or quickly. All of this is new to me. Worse than being called upon in law school and far worse than my first set of exams. I'm a mess. I have been back and forth with doctors. And I checked out OK. No problems; heart, lung, or anything else. They tell me it's anxiety and gave me some pills which simply dull my mind and occasionally induce periods of fitful sleep at night. What can I do? I am lost and in a place I have never been. Please, I need some help. I have never failed at anything, and I cannot fail now." Only then did the occasional tears become sobs.

I was stunned. What do I say or do next? As a mentor, it was a first for me. But why me? It wasn't a question of why have I been saddled with this burden, but why did she come to me? What do I do next? Therapy is beyond my training, experience, and job description. I could recommend professionals at the university or elsewhere; perhaps something already tried. Regardless, she was here in MY office. Passing her off felt like abandonment, if for me, then certainly for her. So I handed her my box of Kleenex, always reserved for students at exam time, and quietly said: "Let's talk some, I have lots of time to listen. So let's begin with this. You say you're having a tough time teaching. Do you think it's because of the manifested anxieties or the perception you and your students have of your teaching?"

Christiana reached for the Kleenex, collected herself, and then waited until ready to speak while wiping her eyes until the stream of tears seemed to disappear. "Randy, I'm not certain. Deep down, I think I am doing a good job, but then physically and emotionally I am a mess, so how can I know? One thing I do know is that I am working harder at this than ever before; if anything, I am overprepared for each class."

"Christiana, do you think the students get that?"

She then paused and smiled: "I don't honestly know how they could miss it."

"Christiana, let's begin with a simple principle of teaching; it's not one hundred percent reliable, but almost. Students appreciate and, when necessary, are forgiving of teachers who are serious about their teaching and work hard at it. Effort and commitment are palpable, appreciated, and rewarded. You can't succeed without it. You say that the students see and know your effort and hard work, but do they also witness your gut wrenching anxieties?"

"Randy, not really. That comes later in the day."

"Christiana, and now the big question. Then why the anxieties? Most people have a strong sense of the answer to these kinds of questions; they just need some time to talk themselves through it and someone to listen. And I'm ready to listen. You could begin with something I don't already know from your vitae. But before you share, let me share something with you that, except for my wife Berke, others do not know. I have had my moment too. My very first class. I was prepared, even overprepared, just like you. The bell rang, I got up to the lectern, looked down at the class, and then ... and then I froze. The thoughts were in my head, but I could not let them out. So I muddled my way through the syllabus, said something about expectations and goals, and then told them we would get down to business tomorrow. And then I walked out. Now how about that!"

"Randy, I never would have guessed. That's not consistent with your reputation. Mr. Cool, always in complete control of every class taught."

"Christiana, everyone has their little and big moments and secrets, but the important thing is to get through it, and obviously I did, thanks to Berke. Berke is a realist and can, by sheer force of will, get herself through most adversities. 'Randy, you have no choice, we have made a move for you to teach, and you can do it. I want you tonight to stand up and rehearse everything you had wanted to say and do.' And I did it then, and the next day in class as well. Of course there was a sleepless night in between."

"Randy, was that the end of your bout with classroom fear? I certainly wouldn't wish to live with what I have and you had for very long."

"Christiana, fear is a constant for conscientious teachers, not paralyzing fear, but a kind of fear nonetheless. I have seen only one teacher in my time leave because of paralyzing fear. He felt it immediately and knew teaching was not for him. Continuing was hopeless and a mistake that had to be ended. But paralysis is not the norm. A good teacher wants to do well in the classroom, and beyond. Daily! And that's always a challenge. You have to be on top of your game, always thinking ahead. Where you are going and how you are going to get there. One must be clear-headed and quick-minded. Like an athlete confronted with a big game or match, there is always nervousness that disappears once the class begins. Honestly, when it's not there, I really begin to worry. But it doesn't stop there. Over time, there are other matters, especially as one gets older and reaches my point in life. If you have established a good reputation, one always wants to preserve it. Each school year one wonders: with the new group of entering students, can I recreate my reputation and the good will that accompanied it? A conscientious teacher questions this, because teachers know reputations are fragile, even good ones. No one slides by with a free pass. And the greater the gap in age between students and teachers, the more vulnerable reputations become. I have witnessed outstanding reputations disappear in a flash because of both big and little things, sometimes well beyond a teacher's control. And as one gets older, everyone slips a little. No one is ever as quick or agile of mind. No one is immune. At some point, everyone wonders: did I say this before? Or after distraction or diversion: what had I wanted to say? And teachers know it and fear the consequences of not being quite the person they once were. In other businesses, one might be let go and replaced. These kinds of casualties are commonplace. But with tenure and no mandatory retirement, old teachers don't usually disappear. They keep on going. For most who have worked hard for a good reputation, their student evaluations remain intact. But slippage is inevitable. When will it be too much; when must I give up something I love? I once had an older colleague — who was an all-time great teacher — tell me: 'I am not nearly the teacher I once was. The students don't know it, but I know it. And it scares the hell out of me to know that they may discover it at any time.' Christiana, worry and fear are constants in one form or another. They are inescapable for someone who really cares. That's life, and it's something livable. But I have said more than wanted and delayed your response to my big question. OK, Christiana, now it's your turn to share."

"Randy, why the anxiety? That's the question. And you want me to begin with something you don't already know. To begin with, my roots in America probably go back further than yours. For you, I am guessing early twentieth century, but mine go back to late eighteenth. On my maternal side, I descend from slaves and the plantations of Georgia, and I am the first college and law school educated person in my family, not educated, but formally educated. Early on, many of my ancestors learned to read and write, which was always a well-kept secret. And they told stories that have passed on to every generation. Many continue to live on the plantations in which their ancestors were enslaved, sometimes in houses, even shacks, which go back many years. The land still not theirs, they are there at the will of the owners. My immediate family moved a generation ago, and I grew up in Charleston, South Carolina. My parents are well-read, high school educated plus two years of community college, hardworking, and very supportive of their only child. I appreciate and respect my heritage, and I am indebted to my parents. They have made my life and career possible. A lot is at stake for me. I simply cannot fail as a law teacher, a life beyond my imagination and theirs."

"Christiana, that's a lot of pressure to succeed. Don't you think that's the answer?"

"Randy, ordinarily I would say no. I have always pushed myself. I have always been filled with high octane motivation. I have always believed I was born with a mission and an obligation to take giant steps and become a first for my parents and ancestors. I viewed this as an honor, never a burden. And the path I took I was good at, especially law school and the law. And I wanted to go as far as I could, and to me that meant brilliance as a teacher and scholar. In my mind, that meant both prestige and unparalleled influence on people, both the present and generations yet to come."

"But, Christiana, the playing field is different. You want to excel at something you've not previously done, and you want to do this without direct experience, and you want to do this at the outset. And probably your images of success are the best teachers you have witnessed. Quite a mission, even a burden. And you wish to accomplish this overnight and without anxiety and other costs or dues. I have a suggestion. Why don't we take a time-out and re-sume next week. I am not saying like most psychiatrists, your time is up. Instead, let's give your anxiety some breathing room and see how you feel next week."

"Randy, but I am not sure why this discussion ends so abruptly, especially with my answers to your big questions. You have gotten me started and think-ing. I'm prepared to continue."

"Christiana, you have given me and yourself a lot to absorb. I'm just won-dering whether you have said enough for your situation to improve without more. And I would like to find out by waiting a week." And so we did.

As expected, Christiana reappeared after seven days, returned to the chair she had occupied, moved the box of Kleenex over to her, and sat in silence. So I began. "Christiana, please bring me up-to-date. Any better, the same, worse?"

She took a deep breath: "Actually worse. You can add nausea and occasional vomiting, sometimes before class, sometimes after. I still need help. I am clueless at this point and also desperate. Despite my determination and desire to succeed and never give up, I am almost ready for the latter." And then more silence.

"Christiana, let's begin with the same questions asked earlier. Are you prepared, on top of the materials, and ready for classroom dialogue and the surprises that accompany it? And do you think the students recognize that effort? And finally, do they witness these anxieties or problems affecting you during the class hour?"

"Randy, yes, yes, and no."

"Christiana, then my response is essentially still the same. More specifically, you are doing a good job, there are internal reasons for your anxieties which a psychiatrist might better understand and help resolve, but in time, they will disappear, especially once you are convinced that you are a good teacher. But I have a suggestion, let me visit your class and observe for myself."

"Randy, that's crazy. You in the classroom? I'd be so self-conscious; I might freeze and shut-down altogether. My answer is NO, that's unacceptable. What made you think I could say YES?"

"Christiana, a matter of trust. I have attended a lot of classes of colleagues, and I think I can see and detect many things and with it confirm your answers to my questions. Further, I can sit behind the last row of seats, and remove myself from your sightline. And still see all I need to see. So please think about it, and let me know whether and when you want me to attend class next week."

After Christiana left my office, some guilt immediately surfaced. I hadn't been completely truthful. Years before I had been asked separately by two entry level teachers — Richard Jackson and Mary Wilson — to visit their classes and help them get through problems that had arisen with student evaluations of their respective classes. Both were in their second year of teaching, both were dissatisfied with their evaluations, and both wanted to improve significantly student commentary and also student numbers to standardized questions that were a huge part of their evaluations. Both teachers were Caucasian, came from privilege, exhibited much confidence, attended outstanding colleges and law schools, clerked for federal judges, and practiced law for a short time before entering the teaching job market and joining the Eliot faculty. And both were surprised by their evaluations. They didn't like the results and especially what it meant students thought of them. While attending their respective classes, I took copious notes. Richard taught constitutional law and Mary taught civil procedure, but my notes said nothing about the substance of either course. Instead the notes focused on how they taught; specifically, the kinds, quality, and clarity of questions asked, their use of follow-up questions, their approach and interaction with students, how well they listened to students and integrated their responses, and, of course, how well students listened to them instead of multitasking with other matters. I also looked for personality and behavior quirkiness that might turn off students. Afterwards, I prepared summaries for myself and concluded that Richard was the better teacher, and that in time, his evaluations would surely improve. I gave him high marks for everything. Mary, however, was different. Her questions were not always incisive or her follow-ups responsive to a student response. Often, she took the easy road when discussion bogged down and lectured. And often, she was bold and said things I could never dare say: "Tommy, how could you say that and let me down after we have gone over this principle dozens of times?" And sometimes she would break into laughter following a student's response that could reflect derision rather than praise. For Mary, I was concerned about whether she could ever make the adjustments needed to improve or affect student perceptions that had probably been formed and destined to be passed on and on. These were my conclusions and, with the exception of my last comment about Mary, the core of my respective follow-up conversations. Later came their next set of evaluations and then the next. I was dead wrong! Richard's continued to decline while Mary's began to rise.

But why? Richard asked me to return to class, while Mary reluctantly gave me permission to sit in once again. This time I took no notes. I simply observed and absorbed. And this time I saw things more clearly, and it had to do with chemistry. A dynamic, sometimes difficult to describe, that promotes human interaction and connection. Why do people like someone? Is it something tangible and easily described? What is it that yields warmth and trust? What is the source of the gravitational pull that some teachers have, and others not, or some Presidential candidates have and others not? That Mary had, and Richard did not. And for someone trying to teach a teacher, is chemistry ever something that can be passed on or even changed without substantial alteration of a person and personality that may never be wise to do or even attempt? Mary had that something. I told her and advised her, except for several suggestions, to stay the course. Richard did not, and I worked with him, yet his student evaluations continued their decline. Ultimately, he left Eliot Law School for another law school of lower rank.

For many years, I have pondered the elements of classroom chemistry and searched for answers with handles that one could grasp and assure its presence for each school year, each course, and each class. Not just as a teacher of teachers, but for my own self-assurance. Self-assurance that its presence one year will not be gone the next. As I said to Christiana, teacher reputations are fragile. Big things and little things that occur during a course within and beyond the classroom can disintegrate goodwill and chemistry in a flash. Often with justification, often without. Positive chemistry at the outset of a semester's course that engenders positive expectations usually yields a positive result, reflected in both the work and evaluations of students, even though the teacher often recognizes he was not at his best. And with that positive result, the process is apt to repeat itself the next semester, and the next. But once chemistry is lost and positive expectations shift, recovery becomes difficult, perhaps even impossible. Negatives are passed on by students with gathering force over time.

I once visited with a former student, Matt Becker, who was a very successful personal injury lawyer. I asked Matt: "What makes you so successful?"

Matt replied: "Quite simply, juries like me and trust me."

"But why Matt? What is the secret to your connection with juries?"

"Randy, I don't know, yet I have come to trust it."

But juries don't have the same history driven reputations of lawyers. Lawyers may have reputations, especially those driven by results, but the pipeline never compares to the lifespan of a law school teacher's reputation that lasts a minimum of three years. Instead, a bad performance and bad result aren't in the knowledge bank of the next jury panel. Inevitably, lost Karma becomes another underlying concern and fear of teachers who have enjoyed the benefits of good chemistry. What is it and how can I maintain and assure it? And with Christiana, I would love to witness it and assure her of it. Yet would I know it if I saw it?

Several days elapsed, yet Christiana did not call. Silence. I didn't see her within the building and didn't hear from her electronically. So I simply knocked on the door with my own box of Kleenex in hand. With permission to enter, I opened the door as she looked up. Her expression was one of preoccupation and annoyance. Before she could say anything I simply said: "I am here for an answer, and I have MY box of Kleenex in case you say no to my classroom visit."

And then came a begrudging "YES."

"OK Christiana, unless you select another day of the week, I will see you in class on Friday, although I don't expect you to see me." And then I quickly departed before she could say more, especially about reluctance and change of mind.

On Friday, I entered the classroom before she arrived and moved a chair into the far corner beyond the last of twenty rows of seats. And I hunched over my note pad so that she could not easily spot me even if her eyes went searching. When Christiana arrived, some students approached her with questions, and seemed pleased with their interaction as they returned to their seats just before the class hour began. Christiana was all business except for several successful efforts at self-deprecating humor. The pace of the hour was rapid and electric. I watched her and the students carefully and I listened intently. Her questions were outstanding, and her responses were even better. She smiled and so did the students around me. Throughout the hour their attention was intensive and unwavering. Eyes dropped down only when notes were being recorded. There was palpable warmth flowing in both directions. I saw it, I knew it, and I embraced it. At the end of class students ran up to ask questions and to absorb everything Christiana had to say. I soon left the classroom with the answers to my questions and with it a sigh of huge relief.

Fifteen minutes after returning to my office, Christiana knocked on my door, opened it without asking, sat down in the same chair at the same table, reached for the box of Kleenex, and pulled it closer to her. I returned to the same table, sat down in my same chair, reached for the box of Kleenex, and pushed it away from her. "Christiana, I don't think you need this now and, perhaps, ever again when it comes to teaching." She looked at me with skepticism all over her face. "Christiana, your class was a masterpiece for a beginning teacher and for a veteran alike. Your orchestration of the class discussion was pitch perfect. I could go on at length about the substance of what you did. But none of it would have mattered without rapport with the class as a whole and with each individual you engaged and challenged. You connected. You have classroom chemistry. You can't bottle it and I can't readily teach it. Although as a visitor it's sometimes difficult to recognize, I could make no mistake today. It permeated everything you did and said. Bravissima! Now tell me how you felt before and during class today."

Christiana once again reached for the box of Kleenex to wipe away tears that had begun to show. "Randy, these are tears of joy and relief. Somehow I needed to know, yet given my anxieties and physical symptoms, it's still hard to believe. I have been awake since midnight, which probably began with knowing you would be present in class. I could not keep down the little breakfast I had and could barely breathe before and during class. Yet I got through it with anxieties and symptoms that failed to interfere and even went undetected. Randy, I am grateful. Thank you."

"Christiana, are you ever exhilarated by moments within or after class?"

"Randy, NO, I have been preoccupied simply with getting through each hour without choking and freezing up or vomiting."

"Christiana, I am confident that exhilaration comes next followed by exhaustion. The highs of a good class hour are enormous and electric, and the lows of exhaustion reflect the extraordinary effort, concentration, and intellectual challenge of a well-orchestrated class. These are the rewards and price of a dedicated teacher, someone you are now and will always be. What you have just accomplished is very impressive. Many people would not have been up to it. But you persevered. I am proud to know you. And I THANK YOU."

Christiana's symptoms did not disappear immediately. Her nausea disappeared and within a month her blood pressure returned to normal. But she continued to wheeze and was short of breath. These symptoms became less at the end of her first semester of teaching when she received her student teaching evaluations that fully confirmed her excellence and everything I had witnessed. And they disappeared completely by the end of the school year when her evaluations confirmed that she was, as a first year teacher, right up there with the best of Eliot's faculty. That summer she began and completed her first article, which was published by the Harvard Law Review. It was a break-through piece on privacy that earned her instantaneous praise and interest by other law schools. Though overwhelmed by her immediate success, Christiana was up to the challenge. Within two years, she had published another article and a book, both on the legacies of slavery, and was off to join the faculty at Harvard Law School, where she is today as perhaps their brightest star.

It's been nineteen years since Christiana showed up at my office. We have visited briefly several times at conventions and exchanged a few e-mails. But nothing more until today when I received the following letter.

Dear Randy,

I am now age forty-six, too young to be on the downhill of teaching yet not too old to remember and value the time we spent together many years ago. I remember well what you did for me, but most of all, everything you said about teaching and life.

I am a dedicated teacher. No longer afflicted with high blood pressure, nausea, or wheezing, but I am nervous before every class followed each day by exhilaration and exhaustion. And before each semester I am especially nervous—and even terrified before the school year begins—as I hope to repeat success of the past. It is, as you once said, the price of perfection, a desire to improve, and the fear of lost Karma. It is also the price of always wanting to hold on to what I have been. The more I teach, the more I learn about teaching, and the more I am concerned with the elements of chemistry, its fragility, and how to preserve it. I have seen others struggle and even lose it. Holding on may never be possible once I begin my downhill journey in life. But I am a teacher and will do my best until I can no longer. Meanwhile, I will revel in the exhilaration and appreciate the exhaustion that accompanies a job well done.

Best wishes,

Christiana

OF STUDENTS

As I said at the outset, the fears of law school students are many. Initial fear of the classroom experience has been uppermost. But these days, especially since the recession of 2008 when law firms were hit hard and life as they knew it changed dramatically, fear concerning a job has probably displaced classroom anxieties at the top of the charts. More specifically, up front, it's fear concerning landing a job with income sufficient to pay down mountains of student debt. But that fear is always grounded upon first-year success as a student, always a predicate to high paying jobs. Examination performance means everything. But the precursor for self-assessment and exam prediction is always perceived to be classroom performance. Inescapably, it's always there, even if only a matter of pride.

This tale of student fear is a story of success at overcoming it. Tales of students leaving law school because of fear, unhappiness, or self-recognition of better life choices are numerous and legendary. Every student remembers the classmate who disappeared after one month, one week, or perhaps merely one day. And every teacher recalls the many students who shared personal distress with "confrontational and adversarial" interrogation and dialogue. Often it was not something they expected, wanted, or appreciated. Anxieties and sleepless nights weren't worth it. Sometimes there were better things they really wanted to do, but mostly they didn't know but wanted to find out. And so they did. Sometimes I would hear from them years later. By my count, most are doing better than just OK, and all are much happier. I could tell these stories; although numerous, they are much the same. Besides, I am always attracted to success and the courage to overcome.

My story of success occurred long before the legal market turned on end and before student debt typically exceeded $100,000 for nearly everyone. It was 1978–1979 when times were better for students and very good for law schools. Although the pecking order for good jobs — jobs with prestigious firms, good pay, and on-campus interviews — were grounded on grades, the stakes did not seem quite as high as thirty years later. But student fear within the classroom was the same, perhaps even heightened. A kinder gentler generation of teachers had not yet emerged, and insults sometimes accompanied teacher comments to failed student responses. "That's the dumbest thing I have ever heard." "What an idiot." "With this kind of performance, you'll never make it to graduation or even the second year." Being called upon was inevitable, and weak performance invited scorn. This tradition was boot camp preparation for even worse humiliation from judges who could say anything without consequence. For a student to say "I'm unprepared" was unthinkable; always better to fake it. To say "I pass" ("please call on the next person") was impossible, at least not until it became fashionable at many schools years later. And when I arrived at the Eliot School of Law, if two people announced unpreparedness during a class hour, or even one "passed," either the teacher would pack up and leave or he would ask the student to close the door quietly on the way out. Opting out of preparation or performance was not an option, although out of law school was. With this history, I was astonished to receive a call from our associate dean, Lou Robbin, about a first year student who didn't want to be called upon to recite in my course on Property.

Property was a one semester course which was offered that year in the spring semester. After reaching me, Lou came up to my office immediately. "Randy, I have a favor to ask. Marc Baron is enrolled in your Property course to begin in four weeks. Marc is a long-time friend. He is in his early thirties, has been a successful businessman in Eliot City for ten years, and he very much wants a law degree. Although Marc has given many presentations in business, in class he freezes up, is petrified, and can't sleep at night. Will you please help him out with a semester-long pass at class participation?"

"Lou, you know I have never done that. And you also know I respect—not abuse—students having difficulties in the classroom. Sometimes I back off or at least back up in the analysis underway, but I eventually return with the expectation that there are always questions that yield a successful dialogue."

"Randy, I know that, but he is desperate and is my best friend from childhood. Would you please meet with him?"

"Yes, of course. Lou, have him call me or simply knock on my door. I will be grading exam papers every day for the next week."

At mid-morning the following day, Marc knocked on my door and introduced himself. I welcomed the interruption from grading and motioned for him to sit down at a table where I typically met with students. I explained to Marc what I knew as a result of my conversation with Lou, and I asked him to tell me more about himself and why he enrolled in law school. "Professor Mann, the short story is that I am from Eliot City, went to the University of Pennsylvania for college and double majored in economics and history. After graduation, I returned home, entered the family business (import and wholesale distribution of musical instruments) and quadrupled the sales in ten years. I knew that I was good at what I had been doing, that the business offered other challenges and opportunities for growth and expansion, and that I could make it my life's work, but something was nagging at me. What else was out there that might interest me more? Law school and the law always seemed an obvious choice. Given my ambitions for the family business, at the very least it would give me a new set of analytic tools and knowledge to navigate its growth. That's it. But I really want to talk about my problem in law school because I need your help; no, I need your consent."

"Marc, so please continue."

"I have never ever come close to what I now experience every time a teacher calls upon me to recite, or when I raise my hand with an answer to a question and what I suffer when the teacher follows up with more than expected. I simply freeze, almost as if my mind goes blank and I am an observer of my helpless self within an out of body experience. I can't explain it beyond that, nor can I explain why. I have made many successful presentations, some for more than an hour and all with questions and answers. Never a problem, not once! I know there is a difference. I was in control and could anticipate most everything. But in law school, I am never in control and can anticipate nothing. It's a lot of uncertainty, especially when no response ever seems right."

"Marc, do you recognize that there are others in every class who struggle with the same thing, but they do persevere?"

"Yes, I am aware of that, but I know myself. I also know I am older than most in the class, and I have neither the time nor inclination for sufficient therapy to get me through this. Thus far, I like the substance of legal education, but I can't cope with the process. Once I have a law degree, I do not foresee a career in litigation. I'm a business man, and I don't need a litigator's preparatory classroom jousting."

"Marc, let me think about this. But meanwhile, have you purchased the case book and received a copy of my syllabus? If you have, please come by tomorrow morning prepared to discuss the first case, *In re the Estate of Sullivan*. Just you and me, just the two of us. No room full of eighty or more students."

"Professor, yes I have the materials and I am willing to try that, but why?"

"Marc, trust me, I always relish an experiment."

The next morning, Marc came by at 9:30. My door was already open, so he entered and sat down in the same chair, and announced that he was ready to begin. I left my chair and desk where I had been grading, took my copy of the casebook and notebook containing my teaching notes and set them on a lectern that I had retrieved from a classroom and already placed on the table where Marc was seated. And then I immediately began: "Mr. Baron, please tell me about the facts of *In re Estate of Sullivan*." Marc was stunned and seemed to freeze. So I repeated myself with, as best as I could, an attitude of respect and patience. His face turned pale. "Marc, this exercise is not for real with others around, but trust me it is for real regarding your future. Just give me something, anything, especially facts that immediately come to mind. And I want you to relax and think until something comes to mind. So do not give up! I am just going to wait and wait until you tell me something."

And I waited, and I waited until Marc KNEW it was for real and knew he had to say something. After a time he began: "This case involved real property owned by John Sullivan who died without heirs. Accordingly the land escheated to the state of Nebraska pursuant to a statute consistent with the common law." Then Marc stopped and seemed unable to continue. And so I waited once again as a look of desperation took over.

"Marc, talk to me, talk to me. What's going through your mind? You may think it's blank and frozen, but I know something is rattling about. Like — 'Did I say something stupid or wrong?' 'What does he think?' Well, Marc, it's not something wrong or stupid, it's a good beginning. Now talk to me." And then, he smiled.

"Professor, your reputation precedes you. You CAN read minds."

"Marc, some say law school is a game of reading minds, students struggling to read the minds of teachers, and teachers doing the same. But let's continue. You said there was a statute that governed escheat. What were the prerequisites to an escheat?" Marc replied one must die without heirs. I then asked him to give me an example of whom he thought might qualify as an heir, which he did. "OK Marc, now suppose John Sullivan had died without heirs leaving his entire estate by will to you. Would the real property have escheated to Nebraska?" No response, but no look of desperation either. "Marc, talk to me. I'll bet the wheels are turning this time."

"Professor, I'm trying to sort this out."

"Marc, let me help. What's the title to the statute that governs escheat?" And then a broad smile as the light bulb turned on.

"Laws of Intestacy, Professor. Without a will. Another prerequisite to escheat. I would take everything!"

"Bravissimo, Marc. I think we have accomplished a lot, and I have a proposal with a question you need not answer today, but should be answered before the semester commences. Today you have demonstrated that you can engage and participate in a dialogue with uncertainties that demands careful and patient analytical thinking. Yes I know it's just you and me, and I know I led with a strong hand in which I spoon fed, but I always do in every class. I try to lead and accomplish something positive for the student and the class. The only times in which I try to mislead, confuse, and break down is when a student has given me unexpected perfection and I wish to determine whether their reply reflected brilliance or calculated guess-work. I am convinced that what I witnessed today can be replicated in the classroom, at least eventually. I am going to give you two choices. In my syllabus, you have undoubtedly discovered some course rules. One tells you about the expectation and requirements of preparedness and attendance. It also informs students that the progress and quality of the course depends upon the participation of everyone and is the responsibility of all, and a demonstrable unwillingness to participate in class discussion can reduce a final grade by as much as four points. And that unwillingness can be evidenced by repeated unpreparedness or numerous absences. Now that's one choice. The other is for me to call on you most every day."

"Professor, did I hear correctly — every day!"

"Essentially YES. I can't do it literally every day for two reasons. First, I don't want students to think I have singled you out for anything, especially terror. Second, I must have the right questions to ask. As to this second point, I propose to begin with questions of simple facts. 'Who is the plaintiff?' I will begin with one question, and get you accustomed to speaking out. Some days I may ask a second but similar question. And these questions will ALWAYS occur in the first ten minutes of class. I won't make you wait for the shoe to drop. Thereafter, when it appears you are comfortable with these kinds of questions, I will turn up the intensity with questions that require something analytic, always moving you up the mountain of degree of difficulty. I won't wait for your go-ahead; you'll simply have to trust me. Marc, these are your two choices. I don't expect or even want a reply now. But as you ponder these choices, I ask you to think about this. As I recall, you said your reason for leaving the family business was to discover what other choices existed, professional choices you might prefer. You can't really answer that question if you shield yourself from a process that's central to many of these choices. Apart from the importance of analytic skills achieved through classroom dialogue, you must recognize that all lawyers must confront uncertainty, the absence of clarity, and the need to think and respond quickly and with agility. In short, you don't want to pigeonhole your choices at graduation. So I will see you sometime before the next semester with your answer to my question: action or inaction. Our mock class is over, the bell has rung." I then moved the lectern off of the table, and Marc packed up and left.

Four days later, Marc returned, announced his presence, entered the open door, and sat down in the same chair at the same table. But he did not say anything. "Marc, what's your answer to my question? Yes or no, I need to move on and so do you."

"Professor, I don't feel like doing it, but I am not sure."

"Marc, then your answer is really YES. If you're not sure, then think down the road twenty years. How would you feel then if you didn't try?"

"Professor, my answer is yes, but is there any signal I can give you, once my interrogation is underway that I am frozen and desperate and cannot go on?"

"Not really Marc. Last week in my office experiment, one-on-one just you and me, did you freeze up at the outset? It certainly appeared that way. More importantly, along the way did your frozen state melt enough for you to respond intelligently? Marc, it's a matter of trust. I want you to succeed. See you in class." And then I stood up and motioned for him to leave.

In re Estate of Sullivan was the first case discussed in my Property class, and it occurred on the second day the class met. And, once again, I began: "Mr. Baron, would you please tell us about the facts of *In re Estate of Sullivan*." And again Marc appeared stunned as his face quickly lost color. So I waited. Slowly Marc took a deep breath and began as he had begun before but this time said more about escheat, its common law history, and it prerequisites under the Nebraska statute. Then he came to a screeching stop, and I knew it was time to bring someone else into the discussion, which I did, and so I released Marc for the remainder of the hour. Yet I also knew this case offered plenty of opportunities to involve Marc over the next two weeks. *In re Estate of Sullivan* was a teacher's dream. My ambition, never realized in over fifty years, was to teach the entire course with just three cases, with *In re Estate of Sullivan* among them. The opinion in this case was less than two pages, but to understand it, one had to master cornerstone concepts in the law of property and, once mastered, first-year students had the conceptual framework to understand and apply sophisticated estate and gift tax provisions within the Internal Revenue Code. My two weeks on the case became legendary over the years—nearly all teachers covered multiple cases per class—but I always considered merely two weeks insufficient.

The following day, I called on Marc to explain something more about escheat and its origins which students had learned from supplemental assigned readings, and he got through it with some stops and start-overs. But he did it and then smiled. And the next day, more of the same, essentially straightforward recitation of specifics that did not require analysis and application. By the time we arrived at the second week, I felt that Marc had become comfortable hearing himself speak out, and so it was time to take a chance and increase the degree of difficulty. We had already discussed and established the court's rationale for its decision, and it was time to test the class's ability to apply that rationale to a series of hypothetical questions to determine just how well the rationale and its underlying concepts were understood. Essentially all of the hypotheticals, some planned and many on the fly, did not involve an escheat. Instead they involved issues and problems beyond the context of the case itself. Yet the rationale and reasoning of *In re Estate of Sullivan* empowered the class to address and resolve each of the hypothetical questions. And I expected this exercise to take two days of class time.

The first several hypothetical questions were straightforward and easy, and the rest progressed dramatically in degree of difficulty. So I began with "Mr.

Baron." Marc breezed through the first three, and then I moved to someone else. Several examples later I returned to Marc, and he did not hesitate with his answer. So I asked him to explain further. He then elaborated his understanding of the rationale and controlling concepts that reflected consistency in his responses to each of the questions he had addressed. I then asked Marc how he would respond to the intermediate questions asked of others. Again, he had thoughtful answers that reflected consistent analysis. We continued the next day with more hypothetical questions. As we neared a conclusion, I presented a question designed to challenge the ability to think beyond known horizons. Up went Marc's hand with a response. Although his remarks tied together all of his answers and presented a viable understanding, it was not the correct one. But it reflected an anticipated common misperception that reared its head in previous classes. Most of all, Marc had demonstrated his ability to grasp an underlying principle and apply it within a known context and beyond. And he accomplished it without freezing up in front of others. When finished, he smiled and then I smiled. "Mr. Baron, although wrong, very well done!" And then we both smiled.

Later that day, Marc came by my office, knocked on the open door, entered as I looked up, sat down in the same chair at the same table, and grinned. "Professor, thank you. Thank you for everything, especially for not saying yes to my request for a semester long pass in class. I think I can do it now, on my own and without your set-up questions in class."

"Marc, I think you are correct, you can do it and on your own. I am very pleased that you accepted my challenge, many would not. So I will see you in class and look forward to your contributions both big and small. But do stop by with questions or most anything you wish to discuss. And now I have to prepare for tomorrow." Marc then left my office and graduated from law school at the end of his three years, but he did not leave my life or the law school family.

Marc returned to the family business and dramatically changed it from the import and distribution of musical instruments — mainly classical — into modern times. Translation: rock music. With manufacturing plants in China and the United States, his company has become a preeminent maker of guitars and amplification systems. And throughout, Marc has remained connected. We have lunch regularly to discuss anything and everything. He serves on the law school advisory board and is one of its leaders. He also loves to address law school students, collectively and individually. And his message is always about how a legal education, and especially its Socratic method, is wonderful preparation for a career in business. But with me, Marc gets very specific. "Randy, sometimes I wish you could peer over my shoulder when I am negotiating a deal or talking to lawyers. I'm always searching for the right questions because they illuminate the strengths and weaknesses in strategy, positions, and arguments, and when I find them, I wish to probe and probe some more. I want to understand, and I want to know the 'why.' I want to reason my way to a sound footing. Randy, if present, you might see yourself in me. You would observe what you have given to me, and sometimes even find me playing the role of Professor Mann. And I love it."

Many years have passed since my experiment with Marc Baron. It was my first serious attempt at overcoming student paralysis in the classroom. The effect on me was profound. Immediately, I became more conscious of what was happening to individual students during the course of a Socratic interrogation. For one thing, I found myself leaving the lectern to move closer to the student under fire. And I watched carefully for all forms of body language. The eyes especially as I searched for contact, redness, and sometimes tears. And I listened. Mumbled or even inaudible words could tell me much. Anything. And when the markers were there, I often initiated with a quiet meeting outside of class in my office where I got to know the student better. Sometimes it was nothing, I was simply mistaken. Occasionally, personal problems were the cause. But often it was a variation of the paralysis seen before in Marc Baron. But just as often, students came to me because of the Baron paralysis pleading for relief from class participation but wanting help. And so it was time for another Baron experiment, and then another, and another, and another.

Were these experiments successful or as successful they were for Marc? For one thing, each of the students remained in law school and graduated as planned. None turned the corner as completely or as quickly as Marc; some, however, did it over a semester and even became classroom stars. Most simply improved and avoided long-term paralysis that would have driven them from law school or encumbered them in practice. And a few merely survived and graduated. All of it took time and thought. Was it worth it? You bet. After all, I am a teacher.

CHAPTER 8

ABOUT MY FAVORITE STUDENT (AND ALSO ABOUT MY DAUGHTER)

FROM WHOM I HAVE LEARNED MUCH

E. Randall Mann

July 4th, 2015. Rain for the fifth day in a row and no end in sight. Most July rain in the history of Eliot City. Climate change deniers are trying to explain. I sit in my study, look out the window and, although I begin each day hopeful, all I see and feel is gloom. I am enveloped by sadness, something not constant, yet unpredictable and always overwhelming. Unending unyielding emptiness, something not even thirty days of uninterrupted sunshine can alleviate. Berke, my wife of nearly sixty years, is doing better than I am. It's her upbringing—strong, resilient, and never waste a precious day. Life is not about simple existence; it must be lived, always with enthusiasm. That's what I found compelling and irresistible when I first met her, and I still do.

We have lost our first born, our daughter Laura. A month shy of her fifty-third birthday, and her death a parent's nightmare. It came from natural causes. She was alone. I imagine too much, mainly pain, suffering, and no 911. The trigger for profound sadness has been a surprise. Not conflicts growing up and beyond, but good times, fun times. My best memories, without new memories to come. All past tense, no future.

In my mid-eighties, I sit here each day for much too long and think about death and those who have died before me. Parents, grandparents, dear friends, Laura, and especially former students, some young enough to have been grandchildren and many in between or even beyond. All died young. Killed by a car one week into her first semester. Another died of an aneurism during his last semester of law school. Another of a virulent cancer three months after graduation. Another of a sudden heart attack at age fifty-four, another of cancer at fifty-five, and another of suicide at sixty. The list goes on and is much longer than one might think. These students had surviving parents, just like me. I can now understand their grief and sadness, but could not then. It is something unimaginable without belonging to this fraternity no person ever wishes to join. But thoughts of death inevitably turn to life. Can I find meaning in Laura's life and in the lives of my family of students who died much too soon? Perhaps consolation? Inspiration? At least peace? Will this journey help me mourn or, better yet, live again? I do not know. The way to begin seems obvious. With my favorite student.

Who has been my all-time favorite student? I was a teacher at the Eliot School of Law for over fifty years, and as I approached retirement, I heard this question frequently. Actually constantly, especially from graduates expecting me to select them. Berke will sometimes answer the question for me: "All were favorites." Mainly she tired of hearing me say when referring to one of them with whom I had had recent contact: "You know how much I liked her (or him); she is an all-time favorite." And then Berke would add: "Randy, how can you have a favorite child? For you this is no different." Yet I am not sure it's the same. Because, as I think about it, among six thousand former students, there are people who truly stand out because of brilliance, judgment, personality, or success, and sometimes all four. There are people whom I have liked better than others; that's only natural. And there are those who have become great friends. Yet who are the favorites, and what are the stories that make them favorites?

One might think that among former students, my good friends — and there are many — would be my favorite students, and if I could narrow it further, my all-time favorite. Yet as I try to answer this question, I surprise myself with "not necessarily." Students have become friends for many reasons, but the constants among them are not always brilliance, personality, or success. Judgment perhaps, but not always the other three. They have been a diverse group, especially their backgrounds, interests, and life after law school. The making of these friendships has not been predictable; quite simply, they happen. Sometimes they emerge from shared experiences with basketball, tennis, or softball. More frequently, they are borne out of brown-bag lunches and office-hour discussions. These friends often become very good friends, and they have been like family, especially as our children were growing up. I could depend upon them in good times and bad. And I have. Yet I am not sure why they don't readily qualify as an all-time favorite student. Favorite people perhaps, but not necessarily favorite students.

As I search for an answer, I must begin with the obvious: I have been a teacher, specifically a law professor. And a teacher must teach. A teacher must have some impact as an educator. So I ask the question: if a teacher has nothing to teach or impart because a student knows or has everything, how can that student possibly qualify as a favorite student? (I assume, of course, that it's the teacher who recognizes this fact and not merely the student.) This is the simple explanation, but it isn't an adequate explanation, because often the students who have impacted me most have also imparted most. Dedicated teachers recognize how much they learn from students, sometimes much more than they teach. This is a reality often not evident in early years. But it is a reality, nonetheless, certainly for those who are open and listen well. For me, these are the students who impress and mark me for life with their ideas, questions, and different analyses of rules, policies, and all of life. But they also affect me in other ways with their vitality, courage, resourcefulness, and resilience. And it's here that I find the core qualities of my all-time favorites who as students gave me something special that enriched my life as a teacher and beyond. In short, these are students who have overcome something in life. They have climbed mountains that others might not attempt. They have inspired me in countless ways, and I am grateful to have been a part of their life, but even more that they have been part of mine. And it's here that I might find salvation or at least the resilience to live each day in praise of life and all that remains of it.

I first laid eyes on Jack Smith at his first class on his first day of law school. In fact, I couldn't miss him. I arrived at the classroom fifteen minutes early and immediately noticed one person already there. I instantly observed three things about Jack: he appeared to be tall even though seated; he had a full but trimmed beard; and finally he greeted me with a warm smile, quite unlike first year students who typically avoided eye contact for fear of recognition and being called upon, which was always a consequence of teacher recognition. Then I saw the wheel chair. After that, frequent changes of position, side-to-side, a kind of squirming because of impatience (which it wasn't) or constant discomfort or even pain (which it was). I nodded and returned the smile, arranged my teaching materials on the lectern, leafed through them, gathered my thoughts for the first class on the first day, and watched the remaining eighty-four students arrive in groups and one-by-one.

And so began that first class, in August 2002. I didn't call on Mr. Smith that day or the next, but I did observe him both days. Still the smile and the squirming. Yet it was more than a smile, it was expressive. It was a face that told me much about understanding and confusion, about agreement or disagreement, about excitement, joy, impatience, and boredom. This class began my forty-first year of teaching. In my early years, especially with courses taught for the first time, I was prepared barely two weeks ahead of each assignment, and for many years, these assignments each required ten hours of work. And the focus was always on substance and mastery of the subject matter. The method was Socratic — interactive dialogue and engagement that led the class through critical analyses of cases, statutes, problems, principles, and policies. This seemed to come naturally, but only when fully prepared as to substance. But once mastery arrived ten years into teaching, I began to observe more within the classroom and experiment with methodology and technique. The first thing I noticed was faces. People communicate in many ways, and words do not tell you everything. I discovered that I couldn't hear without my eyeglasses. "I understand" becomes meaningless when body and face suggest otherwise. Quite differently, a broad smile often communicates insight and understanding without need for words. When the whites of eyes of someone called upon reddened, I observed unknowing, confusion, and vulnerability, and a need to proceed with careful guidance and patience and sometimes to back-off completely. Faces told me much, and always within each class, there were students, usually very good students, whose faces measured and reflected where the class was at. Consequently, my goals for the first week of class, especially for freshman law students, were to learn the names of students and to identify the faces that became my classroom barometers for things important to teaching. And I knew immediately that Jack Smith was a perfect choice. And he was.

On the third day, I called upon him. "Mr. Smith, would you please tell us about the facts of the *O'Brien* case."

Again he smiled and squirmed, but replied: "Certainly."

That began a discussion that involved him and several other students—but mostly him—for the entire class hour. His responses reflected excellent preparation, and much more. His analytic skills were outstanding. He was agile, thoughtful, and immediately could detect problematic responses and redirect himself and lead class discussion to insight and understanding. A week later, he raised his hand to comment and ask a question. After forty years of teaching, it was a question I hadn't heard before and did not anticipate, and it wasn't my initial encounter with this kind of unknown question. Although I always tried to prepare for everything, every twist and turn possible that brilliant young minds might generate, that was impossible. Early on, these experiences presented moments of fear, and my response would typically be one of avoidance or at least delay: "That's a good question, let me think about it, and I will get back to you." Yet it didn't take long to recognize that these unexpected classroom experiences presented the most exciting educational opportunities for both student and teacher.

For me, these kinds of questions challenged ways of analyzing and solving problems, and challenged accepted policies and legal principles and their application. Further, these questions would trigger new ideas to research and explore, eventually leading to some of my best published work. As to the student, these questions presented the opportunity to turn the question around and give it right back to the student, thus affording the student a teacher-guided experience in critical analysis that would empower them as lawyers tasked with problem solving. And so I responded: "Mr. Smith, now that's a very good question; quite frankly, it's one I never had before! Let's think it through together. But you begin, Mr. Smith, what do you think?"

Without a blink, yet with a smile, he replied: "But I asked first, and you're the Professor. Professor Mann, what DO YOU THINK?" The room erupted with laughter. For me this was a great moment in developing positive chemistry with a class. Good natured humor and laughter generated by a student towards himself or the teacher and not another classmate was a recipe for good Karma. Although the line between impertinence and playfulness was fine and sometimes difficult to detect, early classroom tension during the first year could be deadly, and humor was always a welcome tonic. And sometimes it signaled that the process of classroom engagement and exploration could transcend terror; it could even become fun.

I then continued: "Mr. Smith, but I am THE TEACHER, YOU ARE THE STUDENT. AND I AM IN CONTROL. What do you think?"

With a smile, he replied: "Professor Mann, where do I begin? Help some."
And so I did. I restated his question carefully while breaking it up into several
questions that he would recognize and could begin to pursue on his own. And
so he did. One by one, he examined each question and came to a reasonable
and defensible conclusion. Afterwards, he connected his responses and
provided an answer as to the whole, specifically his original question. I watched
and listened intently with arms folded at my chest. All that I added was some
emphasis, connections, a few questions that tested his understanding of what
he had just said, and summaries of each step he took. Students had been staring
at him, but turned towards me once he finished.

I stood quietly, and then smiled broadly. "Mr. Smith, well done! You have
just demonstrated what legal education is all about and what we are here to
accomplish." And then I laughed and said: "I couldn't have done it better myself." Applause erupted.

Thus began the legend of Jack Smith, in my course and all others throughout
his three years at the Eliot School of Law. Every time I called on Mr. Smith to
recite and every time I recognized his raised hand, the heads of classmates
would begin to drop as they took notes in long-hand or with their computers.
He was always polite, respectful, and measured when disagreeing with his
teachers and especially with other students. And he was always generous with
his time and outlines outside of class, and he seemed almost embarrassed by
the attention and reputation for brilliance that was his. Jack was self-effacing
and sometimes bewildered by it all. I was often surprised by his reaction. Humility seemed quite natural, but bewilderment did not. Given his exceptional
ability, surely he had experienced success and recognition before. Yet the explanation didn't come until a few weeks later.

Jack missed a class. It was a Monday morning. As I searched the class for my
student barometers, I saw his empty place all the way to my right on the aisle,
four rows back from the front. He was absent again on Tuesday, and then on
Wednesday he entered the room ten minutes after class began. I had attendance
rules that concerned absence and tardiness, but that wasn't my concern. I could
not imagine that Jack Smith intended breach of either. Throughout the hour, he
grimaced but did not offer his customary smile. Immediately after class I walked
over to where Jack was seated in his wheel chair. He simply apologized. There
was no warmth, just a grimace that morphed into a scowl. Instead I smiled: "Mr.
Smith, no need to apologize; that was not why I came over. You always contribute
beyond your responsibilities as a student. Most important, are you OK?"

He paused for a moment and replied: "No Professor Mann, I have problems, and I am not good." He then turned to pack up his materials and be on his way.

Every semester, there are a few students in serious distress. Some because of life threatening injury or illness, personal or among family and loved ones. Some because of disabilities that prove too much to overcome. Some because of money, especially when it runs out and hunger becomes a constant. Some because of conflict with a spouse or partner or with parents, siblings, or friends. Some because of impending failure, real or perceived. Whenever I discover this, I recognize two principal choices. I am not trained in counseling, but my university offers help from those who are. I am a teacher whose job is to teach, and in this situation, my responsibilities end when I recommend counseling to those in need. Or I can take a chance, initiate with the student, and try to help directly by at least listening. The downside to the latter option has been nothing more than student rejection: Thank you, but no thank you. In the case of Jack Smith, I really did not see a choice. So before he wheeled himself from the classroom, I quietly said: "Mr. Smith, I am available if you wish to talk."

Seated in his wheelchair, he looked up and replied: "I honestly don't know, but I will get back to you."

The next day after class, he motioned for me to come over. After addressing the questions of several students, I then walked the several steps to where he was seated. "Professor Mann, when can I see you?"

"Mr. Smith, how about now?" We then entered the elevator, exited at the fourth floor, and went directly to my office. My office had a large circular table for conferencing with students. I removed a chair so that he could rest his backpack with books and other things and I could sit near him. "Mr. Smith, can I call you Jack?"

"Professor Mann, of course."

And so I began: "Jack, is there any way I can help?"

"Professor, I am in bad shape these days. Obviously, you have noticed the wheel chair. I used to be six feet four and star football player, but Desert Storm ended all of that with some shrapnel that left me a paraplegic. Although the cause was uncertain, kidney failure followed. Every day since my time in the desert has been painful; the pain never goes away and never becomes accustomed. But I also have daily dialysis at home, and for now that isn't working well. In short, I have been absent and tardy because of time in the hospital. I appreciate your concern, but these are problems only I can address."

Somehow I felt I couldn't leave it at that; I had to speak up. "Jack, there is something I want you to know, something you might already recognize in yourself. Your contributions to class discussion are the best I have seen in forty years of teaching. You have demonstrated every analytic skill that the profession demands and you demonstrate this merely several weeks into the first year of law school. I haven't witnessed your writing skills, but I know how you think and the power of your mind. Although there are no certainties in predicting grades, you are as close to certainty as I can get in predicting your success in school and beyond. Please don't give in or give up. If you need help, don't be silent!"

"Professor Mann, I appreciate what you have said. Do you know anything about me other than what I said earlier?"

"No I do not, Jack. I was tempted to examine your file and application to law school, but I elected not. I want to know much about each of my students, but at the very beginning I want to confine it to what I observe within the class-room."

"Well then, Professor, let me give you some further background. I am Native American and a member of the Navaho Nation. Before enlisting in the Marines at age eighteen, my entire life was spent on a reservation in Northwest New Mexico. I grew up in a four room run-down shack with my mother, a younger brother, two grandparents and three cousins. We had nothing. The land around us was windswept, barren, arid, and hostile. Close your eyes and imagine the moon, and you've then pictured our landscape. Water was limited, and so was electricity and heat. My father was long gone by age five and probably dead by ten. But I never knew. Memories are tough ones, especially those of constant hunger for food and change. Work was scarce, and alcohol was plentiful. Many of us were lost because of one, the other, or both. The reservation school house had several rooms intended to educate everyone. Most of us never made it through grade school. But I was bussed to high school in a town just off the reservation, something that simply happened because of football and because I knew I was very smart and didn't want to waste it.

"After high school, I knew I had to save myself and that meant leaving. Further education seemed beyond me and my self-image. The Marines were not. I enlisted eight months before Desert Storm and sailed through training while testing high in everything, especially physical skills, intelligence, and the mindset needed for forward intelligence. I was the perfect scout. And that was my assignment in Desert Storm. I was sent deep into Iraq. I was by myself, dug into a self-made cave underground, peering out and gathering and sending information on Iraqi troop and supply movements behind enemy lines. I was there for ten very long days. Alone. In darkness, dampness, intense heat and cold, and mostly quiet except for wind and occasional sounds of animal life. It felt grave-like. It seemed like forever. Finally, I was ordered to retreat. But before I could escape, a lone Iraqi thought he had found something and dropped a live grenade down the air-hole to my cave. And I am what I am today because of that explosion. After many surgeries and much therapy, I was able to leave the service. I came to Eliot University on the G.I. Bill and scholarships. It was here that my intelligence was truly validated. I majored in math and graduated summa cum laude. My teachers encouraged pursuit of a PhD. But that didn't appeal to me. Something was missing. I think I have found that something in law school. Purpose." And then Jack went silent. I said nothing. Only that seemed appropriate. Jack had said much. We had eye contact for just a moment, and in that moment I saw white become red yet without a tear. Then Jack reached for his belongings, wheeled to the door, opened it, and left with a faint "thank you" trailing behind. I sat there for some time wanting to do something not knowing what. Thereafter, I hoped for another get together in my office and opportunity to say or do anything meaningful — not knowing whether I could accomplish either — but it did not happen in the remaining weeks of the course.

Jack did not miss a class the rest of the semester, yet he was not well. Jack squirmed constantly trying to find a comfortable position that might alleviate his pain, even if momentary. He also seemed unusually pale, which I assumed was a symptom reflecting his serious underlying illness. Most of all, his expressive tell-tale smile was gone and did not resurface. But Jack's performance belied his pain and untold suffering. In over forty years of teaching, it was simply unparalleled. This happened in my class and the three others he took during that first semester of law school. Teachers do talk to each other about specific students, and the talk is sometimes about good things, bad things, or things of concern. But in the instance of Jack Smith, it was simply awe. I also discovered that Jack had not shared his past or specific health issues with others, so I simply left it at that. By semester's end, I was hoping that Jack's exam performance would match up with everything witnessed in the classroom.

And it did. Jack surpassed my expectations and those of other teachers. His answers were models of perfection. They focused on and interrelated principal and subordinate issues, analyzed and applied relevant law and policy, and finally discussed possible results in terms of what might be or even should be. He ranked first in every class, and by a large margin. Observing this, however, is not enough to describe what he accomplished. Eliot School of Law used a numerical scale for grades. Sixty five was the lowest grade and one hundred was the highest. Ninety was the equivalent of an A, and a ninety three to ninety five was usually the top grade. Jack's average for the semester was better than ninety-nine, with two one hundreds and two ninety-nines. And for the two teachers—I was one—who gave him a one hundred, it could have been ten or fifteen points higher had there been no ceiling. And so the reputation of Jack Smith soared as he became a legend within one semester. But his humility, his sensibilities, and his understated ego remained a constant and fully appreciated by all who knew him, especially his classmates. Jack was all of this, but with a considerable distance from others. His smile, and with it his personal warmth, had gone AWOL.

I did not see Jack during the early months of the second semester, but again I certainly heard about him through his teachers as they began to witness the legend first-hand. With the semester winding down, I sent Jack an e-mail in which I congratulated him on all he had accomplished in law school thus far, and I invited him to become my summer research assistant at the conclusion of the school year. I also observed: "Jack, I know that jobs with large firms will be available to you given your performance in class and on exams. And I also know that these jobs pay very well and that you are not a wealthy man. But I do know that my summer project is interesting, maybe even exciting, and that the hours are flexible, the dress code nonexistent, and the environment stress free. And maybe it's an opportunity to recoup, revitalize, and have some fun. Please let me know if you wish to discuss this further."

Within two days, Jack replied: "Professor Mann, thank you. Between the G.I. Bill and my scholarship that awards a significant stipend for living expenses, I don't need a large firm salary for the summer. Without further details, I know this is the tonic for wellness that I need and must have for now. So my answer is a definite YES. Again, many thanks. I look forward to the experience. Please let me know whether we can defer further discussion until after final exams." And with that we had a deal, a summer, and a friendship that profoundly shaped my life.

After exams, Jack and I met for lunch during which I laid out my research project and strategy and agenda for working together. This involved weekly meals as well as conferences in my office as needed. Jack did not disappoint me. He immersed himself in the research, the writing, and the elaboration and improvement of ideas, theories, and arguments. The roles of teacher and student/assistant were blurred and sometimes indistinguishable. His questions and comments sparked and inspired new projects that eventually yielded some of my best published work. But the best times were reserved for lunch. Discussion had no limits. Politics. Law. History. Literature. Sports! Jack was conversant with each. We often exchanged favorite books. Jack loved biographies — Abraham Lincoln, Benjamin Franklin, and John Adams. He also liked fiction — E.L. Doctorow, Saul Bellow, Richard Ford, Wallace Stegner. And Jack informed me that he had begun work on his first novel, although law school had put it on indefinite hold. We never needed an agenda and often found ourselves occupying an outdoor table into late afternoon. Time always went fast, and by late summer, weekly lunches had morphed into semi-weekly. There were also frequent office discussions, mainly project oriented but sometimes something more. It could be anything. It was a joyful summer.

I once asked Jack: "How did you manage to read so much by age thirty?"

"Professor, I have had many surgeries and many recoveries. This adds up to lots of down time. Add to that constant pain in which one doesn't sleep much and sometimes not at all. Reading fills the day and best of all long nights. I always liked to read, and attributed that to my success as a student in grade school and high school. But I did not read a lot and hadn't had broad exposure to books and literature. I picked up the reading habit in the marines and found it an enjoyable way to fill down time, although there wasn't much of that. However, after Desert Storm, I only had down time. Reading anything and everything was a greater kick than alcohol or more drugs upon drugs. It was my salvation and self-education. I learned I could read, comprehend, process, and integrate substance into ideas and opinions of my own. These were my moments of empowerment and self-confidence. Professor, I sometimes wonder where I would be or what I would be if I hadn't earned this wheelchair."

These are some of things I learned about Jack and from Jack. I said it was a joyful summer, but thinking back, this was my perspective. It couldn't have been Jack's, at least not always. His pain was a constant, and so was his battle with kidney disease and dialysis. Yet there was more. Towards the end of the summer, but before his employment was to end, he simply disappeared. I e-mailed him, I phoned him, but could not reach him. After one week of more e-mails and phone calls, I even knocked on the door to his apartment. But there was no response. I asked around, especially among classmates who were taking summer courses or working as research assistants. No one had heard from him, although each emphasized that this wasn't unusual. Jack was popular but very private, even solitary. Two days later, he knocked on my office door. "Professor, do you have a moment?"

"Yes, Jack, any time! You know I have been concerned and trying to reach you. Very concerned!"

"Professor, yes I know. Are you familiar with PTSD?"

"Yes, I have read about post-traumatic stress, but I am not sure if I have ever known someone who suffered from it."

"Professor, you know someone now." And then he paused, waiting for something from me or rallying his courage to share. I couldn't tell which; perhaps it was both. But then he took a deep breath, exhaled, and continued. "I told you about my time in Desert Storm and, specifically, about the shrapnel, paralysis, and surgeries. But I did not tell you about the worst of it. My living hell." Suddenly Jack abruptly stopped. He was noticeably disturbed and ever so slightly shaking. "I have nightmares often, sometimes they are nightly. Almost always the same with slight variations. When they occur, I awaken drenched in sweat, frightened, and weakened. Afterwards, sleep escapes me as I lie for hours in bed thinking and fearful, too fearful to drift off and chance another dream. Thereafter, too tired and depressed for anything, most of all coping with renal failure and more dialysis. The source is Desert Storm, my self-made cave, the seclusion and isolation and their duration, the desert heat each day and the winter-cold each night, the fear of capture and death, the constant danger and daily twenty-four hour vigilance over ten straight days, and finally the crippling explosion. Throughout I am trapped. Sometimes I think I am in a hole with no way out. Other times, I am in a coffin nailed shut with no one able to hear my desperate cries for help. When I am conscious and awake, and the nighttime dreams are at their worst, I am without incentive and certainly hope. Each day is darkness, and my mood blackness, a combination of painful despair and anger that weights me down with thoughts of suicide. Professor, I go through these episodes of varying intensity, sometimes for a few days and sometimes for weeks, but always they are there on the back burner of consciousness."

Then Jack stopped talking, lost eye contact, looked away, and dropped his head while starring at seemingly nothing. Uncharacteristic and unaccustomed silence between us took command. I searched for something meaningful, but could only utter words both awkward and stupid: "Are you improved at the moment?"

Jack was kind: "Professor, I am not certain what constitutes improvement. I am not at my worst, and never worst is a state that never lasts. Yet it is the state in which I can function, the state in which my teachers have seen me much of the time in college and law school."

"But Jack, tell me, how have you been able to cope?"

Once again, Jack was slow to respond. "Cope, I'm not sure. Manage, sometimes not at all. At first I was hooked on denial, then courage, and then drugs of choice, especially pain killers along with an Indian's best friend, firewater. Professor, you've heard about Indians and firewater, at least in the movies. Well, it's all true, and now there is science to back it up about us and firewater. Its destructive force is everywhere on our reservation; in its wake lies my father, his brothers, and even his father. I became a drunk, plain and simple. Until one day. Until the moment that solution became more painful than the problem and its cause. Alternative treatment options weren't great. More drugs, some talk therapy, and support groups. The VA was slow to recognize my problem and even slower to address it. More than anything, I willed myself into moving forward instead of spiraling downward. And the drug that helped the most was education and the process of learning. That has been my salvation, at least it keeps my nightmares in check most of the time. Professor, I wanted you to know everything. This has been a good summer for me; I owed you explanation and truth."

The summer ended shortly thereafter and so did his work as my research assistant along with weekly lunches and mutual sharing. Over the remaining two years of law school, I heard more about Jack than from him. Our contact was limited, but certainly not nonexistent. This followed the pattern of most former students, even those who served as research assistants. Their lives became exceedingly busy with classes, law reviews and journals, and job interviews, often in other cities. During this time, Jack's reputation soared with each new class, teacher, and classmate. He never failed to impress. Jack seemed to have time for everything including the Law Review (where he became editor-in-chief). I once asked Jack how he found time for so much. His reply was direct, simple, and honest. "Professor, what else can I do or enjoy in life except work? Especially work that most nights spares me from debilitating nightmares. Once upon a time, I was an athlete and an exceptional one. All sports were my passion. Not now except as a spectator, but I am a doer not a watcher. Women? I was a marine and a lover, but who would have me now in my wheel chair with kidney failure and daily home dialysis. You once told me that I had become a legend in law school. But know this, it is a lonely legend that I must accept, perhaps embrace."

So I then asked: "Jack, what about a kidney transplant? Couldn't that improve things measurably?"

"Professor, yes. But I have been there, done it, and suffered through colossal disappointment and the pain of lost hope. My mother was the donor. It was a good match. I fully expected success, not failure. Afterwards, I swore never again. Never could I invest in hope and risk failure and psychological devastation. Never!"

From the very beginning—especially that first week with me in Jack's first semester—I mentioned Jack to Berke. And over time, she would hear more and more at supper about him, most of all during our summer of friendship and work together. She once said to me: "Randy, he can't be real. When will I meet this superstar?"

"At the annual Scholarship Dinner in early November," I replied. This was during Jack's second year of school. I made certain we were at the same table and that Berke was seated next to him. Their conversation that evening was comprehensive and constant. Berke was charmed by the same magnetic pull that captivated everyone in the law school. As we drove home, she couldn't help describing him, at great length and detail, the same as if I had never met him.

"Randy, I am going to invite Jack for Thanksgiving dinner along with the usual group. I think he would fit in perfectly." And she did, for that Thanksgiving and the next. Jack accepted both invitations, but within a week, he politely declined. I always assumed it was work or another black period often brought on by holidays and loneliness. I understood, but Berke did not. She never knew Jack's full story, at least not then, and I never knew how Jack spent Thanksgiving, Christmas, or any other holiday. Though I always assumed he was alone.

Sometimes Jack would find me in my office and want to talk. Unlike lunches over our summer together, these conversations never drifted or meandered into pathways and subjects that simply happened and held interest. Instead, these talks always had a purpose. Sometimes a reference or recommendation. Sometimes a contact or information about a law firm. Sometimes advice about judicial clerkships. This was standard stuff for law students. He was also upbeat, especially as he approached graduation and a real job with a large outstanding Chicago firm that he had clerked for during his second summer in law school. Jack was encouraged by faculty to apply for a United States Court of Appeals clerkship, with another application the following year to the Supreme Court of the United States. But he bypassed those opportunities to go directly into the practice. He simply explained that he was older than most students, and that life was fragile and sometimes short, and he wanted to get on with his life's work. And I never tried to persuade him otherwise.

The day before graduation, Jack knocked on my office door. He peeked in and announced: "Professor, there are some people I would like you to meet; perhaps I should say I want them to meet you. Let me present my family and also my extended family." Into my office marched twenty people, the numbers seemed never ending, almost like the classic circus routine of clowns piling in or out of a tiny car. Yet there they were, only six chairs that left fourteen standing. Jack introduced them one by one and said something about each and why he or she was so important to Jack. They included his mother, brother, grandmother, and two cousins. The others were friends, some very close and the rest tribal leaders. In short, this was his support group from childhood to the present. And more, this family was his inspiration. They were all from the "Res," and they had traveled without a stop over fifteen hundred miles in several pick-up trucks. Several stayed with Jack, and the rest were divided among several classmates who were eager to help. (For these classmates, it was a matter of payback for Jack's patient tutoring within and beyond the classroom.)

Once they were settled, Jack formally introduced me. "This is Randall Mann, my favorite teacher, someone I mentioned to each of you many times. He was my teacher, my summer employer, and is, best of all, my devoted friend, undoubtedly for life. He recognized my ability immediately, encouraged me, and listened to me in good times and bad. He is a part of who I am just the same as each of you has been." While listening to Jack, his family faced him. When finished, they turned towards me expecting a reply, something more than a smile of appreciation. I then circled and moved about my small office as I spoke and forced eye contact and shook hands with each, especially Jack's mother.

"I am grateful Jack stopped by, and I am very grateful to have met each of you. At this point in my life, I have taught approximately five thousand students. And Jack is simply number one among them. His grade average is the highest in the history of the school. It is a ninety-nine, with the second highest now ninety-seven. It will never be broken. But he is also my favorite student because of who he is and what he has meant to me. Jack has also been my teacher, especially as to matters of life, living, character, and courage. I have learned much from Jack but indirectly from you as well. We are all shaped by those who come before, especially family. And Jack would not be here or the person I have known without you. Tomorrow at graduation, you will witness presentation of the awards some graduates receive. Jack will dominate the list. Please know that none of this would have happened but for you. I am very honored to have met you."

The next day began with thunderstorms. It had rained for five days before and continued for the next two. Noon was the time for the procession to begin into the outdoor amphitheater in which the law school graduation was to occur. At 10:30. the rain broke, but the cloud cover did not. First to enter was the faculty marshal, next came the dean and ranking administrators, then the faculty, then the student marshal, Jack Smith, wearing his customary warm smile and rolling along proudly, and finally the graduating class. Although the amphitheater was dominated by green, the color of its manicured lawn and new born tree leaves, the rest was dominated by dark grey, specifically the sky, business-like attire of guests, and the academic gowns. Except for one startling exception that faculty members did not see until finally seated facing the guests. Off to the side towards the back of the audience, there was brilliant color emanating from the faces and attire of Jack's family. They were all in full ceremonial dress. Almost as if seated at a military attention. Jack's name was invoked many times by those who spoke. First in the class, best grade average every year, the James Donald Award voted by classmates to the person who exemplified the ideals of all graduates, the best Student Law Review Note, and many other awards and recognition. Often classmates stood with applause, but his family sat quietly with wonder and appreciation. Afterwards at the reception, they sat together by themselves along with Jack enjoying the buffet lunch. Many students came over, one by one and in small groups, and offered very personal congratulations to Jack and his family, almost as if they were paying homage to a super star, which in the view of many Jack clearly was. I had had my own audience, and so I spent my time at the reception with other students and their respective families knowing that Jack and I would remain in touch. And we did.

During the next two years, I heard from Jack sporadically and saw him just once. Actually I heard more about him than from him. His law firm had many of my former students, including major partners. One by one they reported back. Jack was the hardest working associate they had seen. He had moved into litigation, focusing on intellectual property and was fast rising despite the absence of a science, engineering, or computer background. He was a super star in the making, and they were grateful we had encouraged Jack to join their firm. Once again, he was a legend, but this time it was among established, experienced, highly regarded and highly confident ego driven lawyers who were unaccustomed to dispensing superlatives, especially among associates never their equal. Jack's e-mail exchanges were infrequent and brief, and his phone calls briefer. Almost all communications were initiated by me. On one of my trips to Chicago on behalf of the school, I made time to see Jack, and I insisted he give me at least one hour just like old times. We met at my favorite restaurant from previous work days in Chicago and had lunch. It lasted nearly two hours, and neither one of us looked at our watches once. After placing our orders, I got to the heart of things immediately: "Jack, we know each other well. Talk to me. Fill me in. I know about your extraordinary success thus far; it's not a surprise. But Jack please tell me about you."

"Professor, since graduation you have insisted I call you Randy, but I always find it awkward. Nevertheless, Randy, I am doing OK, actually better than OK. I love my work, and I am very good at it. I have found my calling and passion. I love IP litigation, especially the constant challenge of learning and mastering something new that is always exceedingly complex. Quite frankly, it consumes my waking moments and sometimes even those asleep. I know you will ask about my buried alive nightmares and paralyzing black periods that distanced me from others and ultimately life. Randy, I am better. Occasionally they surface, but never when my work is most intense, including moments in the courtroom."

"Jack, this is terrific news. Your success as a lawyer is no surprise, but virtual absence of nightmares and depression is. Can your doctors explain this?"

"Randy, I'm not seeing a shrink or any other kind of therapist. And I am not on drugs of any kind including firewater. I've been there and done it. I know how I feel, and know I am better, and for now I simply trust it without need for explanations."

"But Jack, what about your general physical health and your renal problems?"

"Randy, I am holding my own. There are always issues with dialysis and my general health. It never gets better; the decline is unrelenting, but for now manageable. Someday there will be a crisis and moments of truth and decision. But for now, that's all on the backburner of consciousness. I have accepted the fact that my life will not be a long one, and probably a journey without a companion. It's unlikely someone I would want would want me. One thing I can continue to do is work and work hard. In the time I have left, I am determined to make a mark. Some have called me a legend; yes, I am determined to be remembered. I want desperately to be remembered, not just on the Res but by all who have known or heard about me. I want to be a giant in legal lore. Randy, you must have some idea of what I am talking about. We can't have immortality, but don't we all want to be remembered? Isn't this the true payoff for teachers — the pebble cast into water and the endless ripples it inspires? Don't you ever think in wonderment: who will remember me and for how long? And if not remember me, how many generations might I reach by the direct impact I have upon several? Might it be tantamount to forever? I also want to be known and affect people in a lasting way. And my work is my only way of getting there in the limited time I have. Beyond that, after Desert Storm, while in the hospital for surgeries and nightmares, I recognized that I didn't want to die. I was undeniably alive, and if alive, I must make the most of it. Life is for the living and must be lived to the utmost whatever the obstacles, whatever the setbacks, whatever the challenges. It must be celebrated; that I must."

For the first time, I saw Jack's eyes redden with a single tear descending down his cheek. Extended silence seemed best. After several minutes, maybe as much as five, I thought it wise to move away from things health, psychological and physical. "Jack, I have another BIG question. What makes you an emerging superstar in IP litigation? I know you are very smart and the consummate hard worker, but the field is dominated by people with comparable talent. And so often, you are up against opposing counsel with PhD degrees in the sciences underlying the dispute."

"Randy, I know the answer to your question, and I have received it directly from the people who judge my cases and me. Juries and judges. After my second or third successful trial, the bailiff came over and told me the judge wanted me immediately in her chambers. When I wheeled in, I was relieved to see a smile on her face. She told me that she had some good news. Essentially it was an observation — a very important one — that both she and the jury shared, but she wanted them to tell me directly. It was important to them, and so, even though their responsibilities had ended, they had decided to stay put until they could speak with me. With that, the bailiff immediately led me into the jury room. The foreman began by summarizing what they wanted to say: 'Mr. Smith, you made our job palatable, better yet, pleasurable. We never once felt like fools as we tried to muddle through the science and technical information needed to sort through and understand the facts of this case. You examined and cross-examined witnesses and exacted information in ways understandable by each of us. And your explanations were simple, direct, and ultimately crystal clear. Quite simply, you made facts and information comprehensible along with relevant law. But you went further with the clarity of your application of law to established facts. We are all impressed and grateful.' Other jurors expanded upon this, but the message was similar. 'You asked questions of expert witnesses in the way we might have. You insisted upon and forced explanations that we could understand. You got rid of scientist to scientist, expert to expert, gobbledygook. You made things real and usable. As a result, we think we got it right.' Randy, I am good at it because I am not trained in science. My ignorance is a blessing that I use to advantage. I am a layman, and when I prepare for a case, I have to ask simplistic questions and insist on understandable responses just the same as jurors. And I have to do this without fear of stupidity. That's it. And it's also the best part. I fool the experts and opposing counsel who see me as a bumbling fool and want to make me one. Victory is always sweet, if not intoxicating." With that, all I could do was to smile brightly and applaud softly.

For the next six months, we occasionally exchanged e-mails. But not phone calls until one evening—late for an old man, but early for an associate still at work—Jack called me at home. "Professor, we need a two hour sit-down. Your turf or mine?"

Suddenly alarmed, I asked: "Jack, what's wrong, what's the problem?"

"Randy, don't worry, I'm OK, but I need to see you in person. Your turf or mine? To make this convenient, I will be in Eliot City this weekend to celebrate a mini-reunion with classmates from college. Can you have lunch on Saturday at noon, and this one's on me? Do not tell me NO."

So I simply replied "YES."

Jack added "I'll let you know where." And then he hung up. What could it be? Good news of some kind for sure. Probably early promotion to some level of partnership. This should not surprise me, nor would a significant offer from a competing firm. Might it be an offer to teach? That would be different and unanticipated, and maybe the reason for obvious excitement in the unexcitable Jack I had known. Saturday seemed a long ways away, but it finally arrived.

I arrived early—fifteen minutes—and so did Jack, moments ahead of me. Just like the first time we met, his first class on his first day of law school. "Randy, I have news; it's good news." And then he paused almost as if he expected me to make a guess. And so I did.

"Jack, you made partner."

"No Randy, but it's something much better. I am married." Again, he paused as he saw disbelief in my expression, not disappointment, but a mixture of joy and disbelief. "Randy everything has happened swiftly, and I want to give you the full story. My wife's name is Riya, she is also Indian as in India, which is where her parents are from. Riya is a lawyer, a very good one, and is currently director of the clinic at the Midwestern University Law School. I met her while I was co-teaching a trial practice course as an adjunct at her school. It was destiny from the time we first met, and from that moment, I only hoped she felt the same as I did. We connect on every level, and sometimes we can speak for each other almost as if we were one. She is the most beautiful person I have ever seen or known. And she wanted to share her life with me. Randy, with me! I sometimes cannot believe it."

And then another pause, as Jack wanted something from me. Not actual approval. Jack was always driven by an internal compass that governed most everything, especially matters of judgment, decision making, and survival. But in this instance, he was searching for my reaction. Surprise he expected, but joy he wanted, and he received both. I smiled as I spoke, but then uncontrollably found myself tearing up. "Jack, I never expected this news; something happy, yes, but not this. And Jack I couldn't be happier for you. In fact, more so than any other good news you might have bestowed. Thank you." Jack then beckoned me over to where he was seated, pulled me down to his level, and gave me a big hug.

"Randy, apart from family, I wanted you to be the first to know. Once we made our decision to wed, we wanted to do it without delay. The ceremony and celebration were limited to several members of each family. You were next in line, but we could not expand it without an additional twenty from the Res, and you have witnessed what that's about. Both families were skeptical. I was able to charm and win over Riya's parents, but the jury is still out on my mother and brother."

"Jack, but please tell me about your health."

"Professor, I assume you mean the nightmares, depression, black periods, and time outs from human interaction. Randy, I can't say that they won't return, but they haven't since I met Riya. As I mentioned to you in Chicago, they were diminished in frequency and intensity by preoccupation with work, but the current depression free period has been even better. I can't say cured, but for now, I have the next best thing. Randy, as usual, our get-togethers are all about me; please tell me about you."

"Jack, don't change the subject. Tell me more about Riya and her family."

"Randy, she is extraordinary. She knows me well, anticipates me, and is more than a match intellectually. And she loves me. But you will meet her and judge for yourself, and I promise it will be soon. Her parents are well-educated, they are both physicians, and they live and practice nearby in Chicago. Best of all, they like me and I like them. Riya has one sister, so they have treated me as if I were their son."

Jack had wanted a two hour sit-down, but it lasted longer. We covered everything about both of us. He wanted to know the latest at the law school and more about my writing projects and any plans for retirement. The time went rapidly, and then he left to return to work and was unresponsive to e-mails for several months. This reminded me of the black periods during law school and registered concern for the worst. But just when I was ready to phone former students at his firm, Jack called on a Monday. "Randy, Riya and I will be in Eliot City this Thursday. We need another sit-down. You tell me when and where. Better yet, how about a restaurant near the Eliot University Medical School Complex? We are driving down and can be there by noon. Please say yes."

So I said: "Yes. The Gaslight Bar and Grill at noon."

This time I was fifteen minutes early, as before, but Jack and Riya were fifteen minutes late. I positioned myself to watch for them as people came through the front door. And then I saw them both. Riya was as Jack described. Her beauty was evident in her smile and the immediate warmth it evoked. In a strange way, it reminded me of the smile and impression that Jack generated as a student. The conversation flowed the moment they sat down. Jack said at the outset that he wanted to make Riya an integral part of our friendship, and with that he let her take center stage. Much was covered, especially teaching. Riya was a committed academic and clinician, but she also sought a tenure track position that was not immediately available to her at Midwestern University. And so much of our discussion focused on the job market, interviews, and publications, while Jack purposely remained in the background. After exhausting that, we went on to the classroom and teaching, and I soon discovered that Riya was thoughtful and insightful about pedagogical goals and how to achieve them. It was exhilarating, just like my many times with Jack.

After some time, we finally placed our food order, and while waiting for it to arrive, I said: "Riya it has been my privilege to meet you, and I wish to help you in any way I can, but past experience with Jack tells me there is something Jack wishes to add to today's agenda. After all, since our last sit-down there has been silence, a telephone call, and finally a three day notice for lunch at a location near the Med School. What's up?"

And so Jack began: "Randy, I wanted you to know now, not later. I am opting for life, more specifically a better and longer life. I never thought I would marry, and I certainly never anticipated becoming a father. And soon I will have both. Can you believe that?"

Before he could continue, I replied, "Yes," and leaned over to give both a big hug.

"Randy, I knew you would say that, but now that it has become reality, I have had to address and make some profound decisions. I don't want to be an inattentive, incapacitated or short-term husband or father, something I could never replace or gloss over with work and more work. As a lawyer, I have proven myself, most of all to myself. But now I must and want to become something more. This requires a successful kidney transplant, and that's what we are here to discuss and determine. I already know something about the risks of mortality and devastating disappointment. But Riya, the person who has already made the biggest leap of faith and with the most to lose, has encouraged me to make this choice and to begin the process. And so have her parents, as parents and physicians. They have fully supported us and our choice to marry and have children. We have collectively talked through the issues and identified the risks, but if a team of Eliot Med doctors view me as a worthy kidney recipient, I am ready to proceed. The evaluation process begins this afternoon in one hour and I can't wait." After that, I said very little except to offer encouragement and hope. Riya then went on to affirm and expand on her support, but soon it was time to leave for the most important meeting of their lives.

––––––––––

More rain and continued gloom and new predictions of widespread flooding. Yet as I tell this story, I find internal gloom less. I have tried to capture Jack's excitement, optimism, and hope. It was contagious then and even now, years later. It simply overflowed and swept me up into a belief of many years of friendship to come. Optimism, perhaps a connection. Jack and Laura at most levels weren't alike. Jack grew up confined by a reservation, poverty, and pervasive hopelessness. Laura grew up in a suburban home, with two teachers as parents, and immersed in opportunity. Jack, from what I gathered, was compliant, but Laura was a rebel and a challenge. Jack became a warrior, and then a wounded warrior. Laura went to college, acted and directed, made tough choices, some good, some not. I find differences that offer no universal truths or insights or ease of loss, yet I also discover similarities. Both had to overcome scars, some self-inflicted, some not. Both had health issues, but still death was beyond immediate horizon. Jack opted for service to his country and later to his clients. Laura, after twists and turns, opted for service to people disadvantaged because of poverty, mental illness, AIDS, or abuse. Jack became a legend; Laura made the "A List" of clients, clinical supervisors, and colleagues at social service agencies. In law school and law practice, Jack discovered his calling, a brilliance at solving the complex problems of others. At work, Laura discovered her true gift, gaining the trust and confidence of others, especially those who could not help themselves. People gravitated to both in friendship, while both gave to others. People simply liked them. Both were optimistic, Jack because of marriage and an expectant child, and Laura because of an M.S.W. less than a year away. Foremost, both were good people, something essential to their work and to all of life, and something I always looked for in students and hoped for in my own children. Yet I continue to wonder, in bereavement, why have I been drawn to my favorite student? Where does this take me? I wonder.

Two weeks later, I heard from Jack by e-mail. "Randy, thus far, it's looking good and now appears as if you'll see a lot of me." After two more visits, Jack learned that he had been accepted and that the process of suppressing his immune system with drugs would soon begin. But because these visits were becoming physically difficult for both Jack and Riya, they proposed shifting the transplant surgery and protocol to Chicago and Midwestern Medical School. This took some additional time, more tests, and separate evaluations by Midwestern, but ultimately, he was accepted, and the infusion process commenced. Things were moving more rapidly while Jack's cup of optimism and joy runneth over. E-mails became frequent with updates on everything including the countdown to a newborn child. There were also photographs — none flattering — capturing images of advanced pregnancy and facial puffing from difficult and toxic drugs. Yet still optimism and lots of it.

During this time of waiting, Jack and I spoke on the phone more frequently than before. It was then that Jack mentioned a probable career change. "Randy, I have previously told you that I do not intend to become an inattentive, incapacitated, part-time, or short-term husband or father. And I mean it. Riya and I have discussed a redirection of lives. She would search for a tenure track teaching job in legal education in a city with first rate health care, and I would follow her along with our newborn. I would become Mr. Mom, and she would become our bread-winner, at least until my Pulitzer Prize novel was published. I am ready to leave law. It was a mountain I set out to climb and conquer, and now I want another, but one that grants me accessibility and hopefully better health. I know I can do it; more important, I know deep down that I would love my job as a hands-on father and a committed husband. Randy, I am not asking for your approval, yet I would welcome it."

I simply replied: "You have it, and thank you for sharing. Jack, you are a great lawyer capable of enormous impact upon all you serve and even society and a greater good. But when reuniting with former students, often after many years of distance, my first question is always: are you happy, are you satisfied and content with your life and what you have become? I am always hoping for affirmation of a life with quality. Jack, I could never dissuade you from opting for exactly that!"

After that phone call, there was silence. Finally, an announcement and photos, Krishna Bidziil had arrived. A son. Krishna, an Indian name meaning attractive to all forms of life, and Bidziil, a Navaho name meaning strong. Both names epitomized Jack. He and Riya had given their son a name and a quest, something far better than Jr. More photos followed as the wait for a transplant seemed unending, even though it had been merely a few months, not years. Finally, the call came—at 2:00 AM to report to the Midwestern University Hospital. A young man had been killed in an auto accident earlier that evening, and his kidney would arrive within two hours. The call had come to Jack and two other transplant candidates. All three were to be tested along with the donor's kidney, with a new lease on life for the best match. Jack was not selected, but a month later, he was. Riya's parents quickly moved into Jack and Riya's downtown condo to care for Krishna, while Riya virtually lived at the hospital. The surgery was a success, and despite some complications, Jack was home within two weeks. Optimism and hope prevailed, even though recovery seemed slow and difficult. More photos of Krishna and parents were streamed. Jack's familiar smile was unmistakable.

And then the fateful day. February 15th, 2011. Jack stopped breathing early one morning. Riya's father, an emergency physician, was present and right on it. But he couldn't revive Jack despite years of experience, skill, and wisdom. 911 arrived and rushed Jack back to nearby Midwestern. Nothing could save him. Riya called me: "Randy, we lost Jack. He is gone. He stopped breathing.

My father couldn't save him, nor could the medics, nor could any measure of advanced medicine." Then she broke down and apologized as she hung up. Optimism and hope now gone; the future Jack elected no more. I cried, and Berke cried along with me. And as word spread, so did all who knew Jack.

Not long thereafter, Riya called to tell me that Jack was being buried on his Reservation, and she requested that I speak. A date was set for March 1st, two weeks later. I replied that it would be an honor to be there, especially to speak. The day was bleak, cloud cover complete, and the landscape barren. I was particularly struck by the absence of trees desperately needed to shield us. A strong and very cold wind swept across us as we gathered within sight of the burial grounds, though not in sight of Jack's unmarked burial site. Custom, I was told. We gathered to celebrate Jack, a sizable group that included Jack's mother, brother and extended family, tribal members and leaders — some of whom I had visited with at graduation — Krishna in Riya's arms, Riya's sister and her parents, two of Jack's classmates, one from college and another from law school, and three colleagues from his law firm. I was one of four speakers. The group included his law school classmate and a partner from his law firm.

I spoke first. My remarks felt clumsy and inadequate because of the moment and a wish for something eloquent and profound. I was prepared with notes and even written text, but unprepared for the moment and emotion. I wanted to say the kind of things I had expressed years before to Jack, his family, and tribal friends in my office. That Jack has been my teacher as to matters of life, living, character, and courage. That most people focus on what teachers give to students, but seldom recognize that students often give back much more. And Jack gave me more than anyone, more than a teacher could ever expect, lasting values as to courage, resilience, resourcefulness, and commitment. And then I sat down and listened to the classmate and law firm partner proclaim Jack's brilliance and accomplishments.

But the best was his younger brother, Tom, soft-spoken, hesitant, and awkward, probably because of the pedigrees of those who spoke before. Tom's eulogy focused on Jack's importance to him, his family, and to everyone who knew him or of him in this Navaho community. Tom explained that Jack was our role model. His life and his accomplishments had already begun to shape the lives of at least some. But for Jack's influence, Tom said that he would have never completed high school, gone to college, or become a grade school teacher. And as if he were speaking to Jack directly, Tom looked skyward and said that Jack knew I was a good teacher, acknowledged it, and always offered guidance and encouragement. Tom then concluded with an Indian prayer that always appealed to Jack. I found it beautiful and of great consolation, but I did not ask for a copy. Nevertheless, I recall its ending.

> When you awake in the morning hush, I am the swift uplifting rush
> of quiet birds in circled flight. I am soft stars that shine at night.
> Do not stand at my grave and cry. I am not there; I did not die.

Until the prayer, Tom had spoken quickly and with conviction. But the prayer yielded much emotion, for Tom did weep, for Tom did cry. And so did others.

Later, as we were preparing to leave, Jack's mother approached me. She had said very little when I first met her at graduation and even less that day. But now she wanted to talk, albeit briefly. She took me aside, and sat us both down so that now we were squarely facing each other without the disadvantage of any height differential. "Professor, I am asking you to make a promise. You and I are close in age; neither knows how long we have on earth. Jack is gone, and Krishna is in the hands of others. Riya is a good person. But she is young and attractive and destined to remarry. I live far away and cannot easily visit. Distance has a way of making people distant. I expect that you will have more contact with Krishna and Riya. Professor, I am asking you to be the bearer of stories of Jack, and to share them often with Krishna, so that Krishna will know his father, know him well and never forget, so that Krishna can tell his children and their children. Please promise." And as I held her hand in mine, I simply replied: "I promise!"

Riya, Krishna, her sister, her parents, and I left the next day, and while waiting together for different flights back home, her father broke down in tears. No one could comfort him. Pent-up guilt had been contained. But not now. I sat and watched as both daughters offered love and comfort. Quietly, almost inaudibly, he whispered: "I was there, I was there. I couldn't revive Jack. I am an emergency physician; I have saved thousands. But not Jack. He wasn't like a son, Jack was my son, the same as if of my own blood. I failed my own son." His sadness and guilt were profound, and from what I have heard still are.

We soon went our separate ways, which was in 2011. I have spoken with Riya frequently but have known Krishna mainly through photos and Riya's descriptions and normal frustrations. She is a single parent, chasing a tenure promotion at an excellent law school, with a very smart and rambunctious son with endless supplies of energy, who tries and gets into everything, and then attempts to explain it away with adult-like eloquence and reason. Krishna is not yet five; he is truly his father's son. Following Jack's burial, I have seen Krishna just once as a toddler, much too young to grasp and remember shared remembrances of his father. Have I fulfilled my promise to Jack's mother? Not yet; of that I am ashamed.

The sun has finally appeared, and so has the heat and humidity of July in Eliot City. I have told the story of my favorite student, but what of the loss of my favorite — and only — daughter? I have muddled my way through differences and similarities, perhaps things that can be found with any two people. Perhaps comparisons have led me astray in my quest. How can one possibly compare loss of a former student, or any good friend, to a child? The investment of love and caring of any committed parent is unending, and so is worry. As I approached age fifty, I once asked my physician: "When does one stop worrying about children?"

He quickly replied, "At age fifty-five."

I then said, "That means a little more than five years from now."

And he said, "No, when they reach fifty-five; you must recognize that parental concerns never cease." And for me, those concerns existed in good times and bad, including periods of painful estrangement. But the bond with Laura never disappeared for either of us. With students, the connection always seemed different, even with Jack, because I had to let go. Graduation and separation, always an inevitability, marked a new beginning (and an ending) in which I was left behind as students climbed their own mountains and sought fulfilling lives. Loss of student connection was a natural part of the educational cycle, something a teacher always experiences and can never escape. But the death of a child, that is incomparable.

Nevertheless, I do know this story telling has helped. The focus has been on Jack. Despite depression, despite a failing body, Jack cherished life so long as there was life to be lived. And he always made the most of it, he always achieved value. Perhaps that's it. I must always make the best of it. I can't cheat myself out of life with paralyzing sorrow. There is a time for grieving, but there must be a time for living and enjoying the time one is granted. That must be it. Knowing that and knowing I can move on with indelible memories of joy and sadness, is all I need. I must know it, feel, and make it mine. But can I? Jack could will solutions into action and reality, reason into faith and feelings, and ideas into controlling emotions. He could take something outside and make it inside, embrace it, and live by it. I have always borrowed from things learned from students. This may be a teacher's biggest debt, though Jack would call it a gift.

———————

Friday, the day after Thanksgiving, 2015. The celebration of life arranged by Laura's friends at her favorite Vietnamese restaurant has begun. We have been overwhelmed by the numbers present, best friends, former partners, agency directors, supervising social workers, mentors, colleagues, and even some grateful clients whose lives she had permanently touched. Mainly people we had never met and even some we did not know of. It was truly a celebration of life filled with joy and gratitude. There were several speakers, and the themes were similar and familiar. Laura was a truly a good person and a devoted and giving friend who has stood by many in times of need. Professionally, she was a gifted and perceptive advocate for those in need. She could contribute to diagnostic and treatment analysis and decision making, and she was a ferocious advocate for clients unable to execute small and big decisions on their own. Laura was also stubborn — occasionally to the point of self-destructive steadfastness — and sometimes resistant to help and advice needed to make life easier and better. She sometimes alienated those closest to her, but then she would call with a voice that punctured all disappointment and even anger, a voice made for the stage or commercials to sell anything, a voice that belied middle age and even failing health. In sum, it was important for all to be there, and important for us to join them. All had a good time, and all felt better for it.

Later that same day. I am now back at the hotel with Berke, and we are combing through a folder of personal effects and photos saved by Laura's friends for this celebration which were presented to us. Berke finds a poem, reads it, and, with tears in her eyes, hands it to me. It is simply identified as a Hopi Prayer.

> Do not stand at my grave and weep.
> I am not there.
> I do not sleep.
> I am a thousand winds that blow.
> I am the diamond glints on snow.
> I am the sunlight on ripened grain.
> I am gentle autumn's rain.

When you awake in the morning hush, I am the
    swift uplifting rush of quiet birds in circled flight.
I am soft stars that shine at night.
Do not stand at my grave and cry.
I am not there; I did not die.

Berke, who was unable to join me for Jack's burial, asked whether I had ever seen this prayer before. I said that I had, and then explained. A Hopi Prayer. Jack once told me that, although neighbors, the Hopis and Navahos were quite different and often at odds. But I guess when it came to things spiritual, Jack was ecumenical.

Comparisons of the journey of Jack and Laura I have made. Differences and similarities. I have been there, done it, and dismissed them as a source of inner peace. But maybe I shouldn't have. Laura was at one with nature. She cherished it and believed in it, and relied upon its powers of healing and comfort. She also believed in spirits and things spiritual, and relied upon her own rituals to celebrate life around her. "Do not stand at my grave and cry. I am not there; I did not die." Once again I hear Laura's haunting voice. A prayer, a voice, a mantra for recovery? At core, my life and work have been grounded in reason and logic, not faith. Yet still I answer: Perhaps.

CHAPTER 9

A POSTSCRIPT

Billie Williams

E. Randall Mann died on June 1, 2016, at age eighty-nine. About a year later, I received a letter from his wife, Berke, asking me if I would assist her in going through his correspondence, especially letters to and from former students. I was surprised by the request because he had retired from teaching when I went to work as his summer research assistant, and therefore was never his student, and because we had had no contact since my graduation in 2011. That was my fault and with it lingering guilt. Yet I wanted to say yes, and so I did. I spent two weeks with Berke helping her read and sort hundreds and hundreds of letters and ultimately decide which to retain. She was very grateful, thanked me profusely, wanted to stay in touch, and then sent me on my way back to the Twin Cities, my home, my husband, and my law practice.

Afterwards I couldn't help thinking about Mann, the correspondence, his life, and what it meant to be a teacher. He was a much celebrated teacher. Although the hundreds of letters (to which he always replied) came from students all over the states, and even the world, whose professional lives were diverse and often beyond law practice, the message in each was basically the same. It always included an update on their lives and work, but first and foremost were remembrance and gratitude. From some came additional letters over the next several years, mainly updates that included marriage, children, partner, change of law firms, and even professional redirection and reinvention. But for most, their one letter was their only attempt at correspondence. And after Mann's retirement, there was hardly a whisper, mainly notes of condolence to Berke following his death.

Mann knew and accepted that this was the way of a teacher, especially after retirement. Forgotten was an inevitability. For students in school, it was a mere three years, even though most of the forgotten teachers still rattled around the building on a daily basis. And for working faculty, it wasn't a whole lot longer, especially if there had been an infusion of new and younger teachers. Faculties have a way of moving on. Power is often driven by the center, not the center in terms of politics, but instead by age and experience. Customs, norms, methods, values, and especially technologies change over time, and for the new and younger, the old reflect the ancient and unfamiliar and with it rejection and avoidance. Mann was prepared for the inevitable, accepted it, but never could embrace it.

I have wondered many times what it's like to hold a class in the palm of your hand almost as if at the center of the universe. And to do this decade after decade after decade, and then to reach the end of a journey and with it be displaced and forgotten. Mann once gave me a glimpse. He said there was sadness. No regret, just sadness. But never overwhelming sadness. Sadness and above all acceptance. Borrowing from a well-used metaphor, Mann once told me that over time teachers throw many stones into water that ripples endlessly in the lives of students who imprint others with the lessons they have learned just as he had passed on the lessons learned from Bernard Berenz, the best teacher he had ever known, and Roger Davis, his favorite colleague and mentor. This was his way of making sense of what he had lost; after all a claim on forever isn't so bad.

ACKNOWLEDGMENTS

This writing project began as an experiment in retirement. It was something I always wanted to try, and I enjoyed every moment of trying. But it would never have amounted to anything more without the support, advice, wisdom, and encouragement of others whom I must thank.

First are my former students, well over six thousand. They are the inspiration for everything. Best of all, they have taught me much, and their lessons appear throughout often disguised by context.

More than any other student, I must acknowledge Bruce Oetter, who has read everything and provided insight, comments, direction, encouragement, and best of all, the perfect title for this book.

Two colleagues and one former student have had an enormous role in this project from conception to fruition. Michael Greenfield, my colleague and dear friend for fifty years, has read and commented on every story and could never resist applying his irresistible editorial pen. Dan Keating has been my private cheering section. He has read, commented, and advised on everything including book sales, and has even appeared in one of the stories as more than just a shadow. And Barry Schermer, an esteemed judge and also an adjunct at our law school, read each chapter the moment it was completed and commented within hours with advice that was always constructive and right-on.

I am especially grateful for the support I have received within the Washington University School of Law. This support begins with Dean Nancy Staudt and our Directors of Alumni and Development, Monica Lewis and Elizabeth Kaul. But it also includes colleagues who have been faithful and encouraging readers throughout. Peter Joy, Rebecca Dresser, and Steve Legomsky.

There are four people about whom I can honestly say that this book would not have reached publication without their counsel, guidance, opinion, and effort. Tom Sullivan, a former colleague, dean, provost, and university president, and a dear friend, has believed in this project and the quality of its stories throughout. And he, more than anyone else, has opened doors to established publishers. Michael Kahn, a lawyer and author of many mystery novels, affirmed the quality of the book and presented me with authentic pathways to publication. And Michael Waterstone, an outstanding teacher, scholar, and dean, read every chapter carefully and thoughtfully, and convinced me that the book ought to appear on every dean's recommended reading list for people considering law school, about to enter law school, or about to begin as an entry level teacher in law school. Mark Savin, a brilliant lawyer (but once upon a time, both a student and university teacher of literature and writing) gave me careful, insightful, and useful critiques of chapters from the very beginning. His encouragement and guidance always got me through moments when I was discouraged. Best of all, as the son of Mr. BB, Mark told me that I got his father's voice pitch perfect even though nearly all of the conversations in the story were imagined. Though imagined, the few unimagined conversations still made him the Best Teacher I Have Known.

And a very special thank you to Richard Ford (and Kristina too) who validated the quality of the story most important to me, one that helped get me through a very difficult time: "About My Favorite Student (and also about My Daughter) from Whom I Have Learned Much." Yet even more important, I am grateful to have had Richard as a treasured friend for over fifty years.

Among my readers, I must recognize those that immediately focused on the psychological issues raised throughout these stories, issues that made the stories compelling and even exciting. More than anyone else, they saw stories with an appeal beyond law school and the law. Andrew Becker, Ph.D. Experimental Psychology; Rhea Oelbaum, MSW, LCSW; Carole Simon, MSW, LCSW; and Merle L. Becker, MSW, L.C.S.W. BCD.

Among alumni and friends are those who have read chapters, some or all, and offered positive reviews along with constructive advice that always improved the manuscript. Joan Newman, David Letvin, David Gibberman, Monique Mutharika, Mark and Elizabeth Levy, Richard Rothman, Philip Shelton, Leo and Robin Romero, Susan Mlynarczyk, Ron Norwood, Sheila Wald, Pete Woods, Robin Kundra, Honey Zeiger, A.D. Denny, Tim Heydt, Jeffrey Rosenblum, Sandy Pomerantz, Gina Tramelli, Nina and Edgar Wolff, Joy and

Sid Kaplan, Sheila Bader, Peggy Newman, Clifford Buchholz, David Rakov, Paul Kochis, Audrey Rothbarth, Gene Kornblum, and Sanford Neuman.

Additionally, I cannot overlook Carol McGeehan, the Acquisitions Editor for Carolina Academic Press, who took a chance with this book of fiction, encouraged and supported me throughout, and ultimately became a wonderful friend.

Foremost is gratitude to my dear friend and wife for sixty-two years, Sandi. Without her sense of adventure, persistent coaxing, and gift of persuasion, my journey into teaching would never have occurred, nor would all of the student friendships without her partnership. She is a successful author and has been an outstanding teacher of kindergartners and me. She has commented extensively on every chapter with comments of approval and disapproval. And I have welcomed both because of their quality and honesty.